W9-BWE-686

SPAIN AND THE UNITED STATES

E
183.8
.S7
R83
1984

SPAIN
AND THE
UNITED STATES

Since World War II

R. Richard Rubottom
and
J. Carter Murphy

PRAEGER

PRAEGER SPECIAL STUDIES • PRAEGER SCIENTIFIC

New York • Philadelphia • Eastbourne, UK
Toronto • Hong Kong • Tokyo • Sydney

359117 Tennessee Tech. Library
Cookeville, Tenn.

Library of Congress Cataloging in Publication Data

Rubottom, R. Richard.
  Spain and the United States.

  Includes index.
  1. United States—Foreign relations—Spain.
  2. Spain—Foreign relations—United States.
  3. United States—Foreign relations—1945–
  4. Spain—Foreign relations—1939-1975. 5. Spain—Foreign
relations—1975–   . I. Murphy, J. Carter (John
Carter), 1921–   . II. Title.
  E183.8.S7R83   1984   327.73046   83-19247
  ISBN 0-03-069618-6 (alk. paper)

Published and Distributed by the
Praeger Publishers Division
(ISBN Prefix 0-275)
of Greenwood Press, Inc.,
Westport, Connecticut

Published in 1984 by Praeger Publishers
CBS Educational and Professional Publishing
a Division of CBS Inc.
521 Fifth Avenue, New York, NY 10175 USA
© 1984 by Praeger Publishers

All rights reserved

456789   052   987654321

Printed in the United States of America
on acid-free paper

The research for this book was made possible by a grant
of the U.S.-Spanish Joint Committee for Educational and
Cultural Affairs, Madrid, Spain.

Preface

By any measure the people of Spain have traveled far since the end of World War II—from ostracism to acceptance, from destitution to economic modernization, from dictatorship to democracy. Americans have been more than interested observers of that journal. After five years of political maneuvering, the governments of Spain and the United States concluded in 1953 the Pact of Madrid which provided Spain economic and military assistance in exchange for limited U.S. rights to construct and use military bases on Spanish soil. While ostensibly a set of military and economic agreements, the Pact and its successive agreements have had a much broader influence than that. Indeed the Spanish-U.S. "Connection," now thirty years old, has had a profound influence on the economic and political evolution of Spain. The "Connection" endured only because it was a practical one for both parties. This study reconstructs the sometimes tranquil, sometimes tumultuous progress of the thirty-year connection and weighs its results.

The work has been carried out under a joint research grant to Southern Methodist University and the University of Alcalá de Henares from the United States-Spanish Joint Committee for Educational and Cultural Affairs. At Alcalá, Professor Manuel Gala Muñoz is assessing the impact on Spain of the U.S.-Spanish educational exchange program.

In the summer of 1981, the authors visited Madrid to gather material for their project. During their stay they held discussions with officials in government ministries and embassies, with officials of financial institutions, and with professors at several universities in the Madrid area. To all of those persons, the authors offer their warmest thanks for the time and expertise that was graciously proffered. For Rubottom, who had lived in Madrid from 1953 to 1956, the visit was an especially heartwarming opportunity to renew long-standing friendships.

The authors want particularly to express their appreciation to Ramón Bela, Executive Secretary, and Thomas Middleton, Deputy Executive Secretary, of the U.S.-Spanish Joint Commission for Cultural and Educational Affairs. Their assistance and cooperation did much to make the whole effort feasible. The authors also offer their respects to their friend and associate in the Cooperative Research project, Manuel Gala Muñoz, and thank him warmly for his unfailingly generous support. They hope that they will someday have an opportunity

vii

to reciprocate in the United States the many kindnesses extended them by these colleagues in Spain

Finally, the debt the writers owe to Barbara Babcock for her tireless help in organizing and typing the manuscript must be noted.

Full responsibility for any errors of fact or judgment that remain in the study belongs, of course, to the writers.

R. R. R. and J. C. M.

Southern Methodist University
Dallas, Texas
March 1, 1983

Table of Contents

List of Tables

The United States and Spain, 1946-53

The Pact of Madrid between the governments of Spain and the United States was signed on September 26, 1953. If a comperized model of what Spain was to be like in the early 1980s could have been designed at that time, based on Spain's past record, the predictions would have borne little resemblance to the Spain one sees today. What futurist could have predicted that Spain would have become:

● the eleventh largest economy in the world,measured by GNP;
● the first nation to be admitted to NATO after the original members;
● a likely entrant to a European Common Market;
● the scene of three democratic national elections in seven years, the most recent providing peaceful change from a centrist coalition government to a socialist government.

By any standard, Spain's transition in three decades has been quite remarkable, but the change did not come easily. What has been most surprising has been the ability of Spain's social institutions to accommodate change of the speed that has occurred.

Some observers might argue that the change has not been profound, that the real Spain has changed little and remains more Spanish than ever. Evidence is strong, however, that, beginning about the time the agreement was signed in 1953, Spain began an accelerated process of economic and cultural transformation which is continuing. Being a part of Europe, the Spanish people probably had no other option. No government in Spain could have survived for long without moving the Spanish nation into the modern era. With or without the American connection, Spain would have been forced to modernize. It might have done so at a slower pace; it might have done so with a

1

different partner, or a different set of partners. But who would they have been? Destiny drew Spain and the United States together.

By the end of World War II, Spain and the United States each found it in its interest to give the other a fresh look. The task of review and reappraisal, however, was arduous. In some respects, a more unlikely partnership could hardly be imagined. The United States was at the apogee of its power and prestige. Spain, in contrast, was destitute, hungry, and ostracized. For a decade, American readers knew only the worst side of Spain, the unfolding of the nation's fratricidal civil war, 1936-1939, and then its links with the Axis powers during World War II. To Spanish readers, on the other hand, the United States was depicted as an interloper in Latin America. Under Spain's Hispanidad Program—more dream than reality—many Spaniards had been led to hope Latin America would return to the fold of Spanish influence. Growing U.S. involvement in that area seemed a barrier to this goal. Then, in 1948, the United States government unequivocally refused to extend aid under the Marshall Plan to meet Spain's desperate needs.

Given the polarization of opinion in the two countries with respect to each other, how did a policy of rapprochement materialize? The thawing of relations was a gradual process, an evolving series of initiatives. Each step was followed by a period of adjustment and consolidation. Increasingly, each nation needed the other.

In the case of the United States, hopes for constructive relations with the Soviet Union had been quickly dashed in the years following the Second World War. In rapid sequence, Czechoslovakia succumbed to Soviet coercion, Berlin required an airlift for survival, the Soviet Union achieved an atomic bomb, and in 1950 the Korean War erupted.

Spain, under the Franco dictatorship, was determined to break its isolationist mold and needed new relations with the Second World War's victorious powers. In addition, it desperately needed economic assistance. It was prepared sharply to revise its Hispanidad Program in Latin America so as to embrace the United States with the other nations of the Western Hemisphere. Salvador de Madariaga succinctly summarized Spain's position:

> Spain's natural strategic advantages are such that, if
> strong, she can play a leading role in world affairs; but,
> if weak, she will be the object of attention from the
> strong.[1]

And the Pact of Madrid nicely illustrates these conditions. From Spain's point of view the pact was a move onstage in preparation for the nation to play her "leading role" when time and circumstances beckoned. Concomitantly, the pact was a move by the United States, at the apogee of its strength, to gain access to weakened Spain's "strategic advantages," and for that access the United States was willing to pay an economic and political price.

Was the price paid to Spain too low? Any Spaniard holding this opinion should be asked to examine the viewpoint of Americans and other Europeans of that day, many of whom insisted that the price was too high. United States political leaders faced savage criticism at home, as well as derision from leaders in other NATO countries, for signing the Spanish agreements. Spaniards of the 1980s may not relish the thought, but Spain's unpopularity in 1953, to put it gently, was both intensive and extensive.

The Pact of Madrid was a hard-driven deal on both sides. While the actual negotiations lasted two years, July 1951 to September 1953, the preliminaries had begun at least three years before the formal negotiations. After the outbreak of the Korean War, Spain raised its demands, but as Spanish economic conditions deteriorated, the Spanish need for an agreement intensified.

The Americans paid their price, too. The New York Times editorialized that the country was "swallowing a bitter pill."[2] The American Protestant community, feeling little sympathy for "fascist," Catholic Spain, was "outraged." Britain's Foreign Secretary, Herbert Morrison, expressing a North European view, declared early in the negotiations that any "strategic advantages . . . would be outweighed by . . . political damage . . . ."[3]

At the time of the signing, both governments were restrained in their presentation of the new agreement. This was no doubt because the negotiations on the pact had been long, and characterized by "give" and "take" by both sides. As is typical for a meaningful agreement, neither side could claim total victory for its negotiating objectives. The language of the agreement was practical, brewed in the crucible of reality. Idealists on both sides were disillusioned, but even their criticism eventually was muted. As one respected scholar described the results of the pact, "A coincidence of needs is a stronger cement than mutual esteem and good will."[4]

SPAIN'S POSTWAR AUTARCHY

To appreciate the economic changes that have occurred in Spain since its opening to the West, one must remember the state of the Spanish economy at the end of the Second World War. Little of the damage of Spain's 1936-1939 civil war had been repaired at that time. Estimates made in the early 1960s of the capital losses due to the tragic conflict between Nationalist and Republican forces indicated that 41.6 percent of Spain's railway locomotives had been demolished in the five-year bloodbath, along with 40.3 percent of its freight cars, 71.2 percent of its railway passenger cars, and roughly one-fifth (250,000 tons) of its merchant marine. A quarter of a million dwelling units had also been ruined and another quarter million partially damaged.[5]

Greater even than these physical capital losses were, of course, the human capital losses, for some 600,000 to 700,000 persons are believed to have been killed in the conflict and hundreds of thousands, perhaps a million, more maimed. An estimated 300,000 Republican sympathizers went into exile, never permanently to return. The nearly one million persons dead or emigrated amounted to approximately 4.0 percent of the 1935 population. High proportions of these totals were young adults, so that the numbers alone failed to represent properly the loss in production potential. Many of the emigres, furthermore, were highly skilled or professional people.

Another property casualty of the civil war was the gold reserve of the Bank of Spain which was shipped by the Republican government to the Soviet Union at the end of 1936 for safekeeping. According to the Russians, this account (some 14.8 million grams of fine gold, worth $575 million at 1935 prices) was drawn on and exhausted by the Republican cause for arms, although the propriety of that accounting for the gold claims has never been fully accepted by many Spaniards.[6]

All in all, according to estimates of the Spanish National Economic Council, Spain's real gross national product declined 26 percent between 1935 and 1939, and, in per capita terms, it declined 28 percent.

During the Second World War, Spanish consumers suffered seriously, and shortages of raw materials and equipment exacerbated unemployment and reduced the effectiveness of efforts at reconstruction. The index of wheat yields in Spain averaged only 72.2 during 1941-1945 (1910 = 100), as compared with 128 for the pre-civil war period, 1931-1935, and unusually bad weather in the peninsula in 1940-1941 and 1945 brought near famine conditions. Red Cross shipments from the United States that began in January 1941, together with drawings under a 1940 British loan of $19.2 million and critical loans from Argentina, helped many Spaniards to avoid starvation.

Spanish authorities, with some skill, made the best of the country's shaky wartime "neutrality" and, in the end, not only avoided invasion by both Axis and Allied powers but were able to extract some profits from sales to both groups. Early in the war Spain obtained limited gains from transhipments of oil from the West to Germany until French complaints to the United States in 1943 brought this trade to an end. The Germans, meanwhile, persistently demanded shipments of Spanish raw materials, especially tungsten and zinc, while the Allies engaged in preclusive buying, partly to limit the supplies going to the Axis and partly to encourage Spain to remain aloof from the combat, especially during the allied campaign in North Africa. The price received by Spain for tungsten jumped from $1,300 to $20,000 per ton between January and November 1941, and Allied purchases between January 1942 and July 1943, came to $74 million. Purchases by the Allies finally climaxed in 1944.[7]

When the war's end terminated Spain's opportunities to experience such trade profits, however, the weakness of its economy was fully bared. An international outcast, branded by allied leaders as the sole remaining rightist, military dictatorship of Western Europe, Spain only narrowly avoided military invasion by allied forces that would have toppled the Franco government and changed subsequent history on the Iberian peninsula. As it turned out, the United States and Western Europe imposed economic sanctions on Spain in 1945 (U.S. sanctions lasted until December 1947), and on February 6, 1946, a resolution was passed in the General Assembly of the United Nations calling on all members to sever diplomatic relations with Madrid and to withdraw their ambassadors.[8] In April of 1946 another U.N. resolution condemned the Franco government and on December 12, the United Nations barred Spain from applying for membership in any U.N. agency, including those to which Spain had previously belonged as a member of the League of Nations. Since Eastern Europe's condemnation of Spain was certainly no less vigorous than that of the West, Spain was abandoned largely to its own resources. Well-publicized loans from Argentina, in an arrangement negotiated between General Franco and General Peron, constituted Spain's chief external assistance in this period.

It is worth noting that the autarchic trade policies of Spain's Primo de Rivera government of the 1920s—policies that had been aimed at a protected development of Spanish industry and that doubtless impaired overall Spanish economic growth in the 1920s—proved to have, after all, some value in the context of the Second World War and its aftermath. The fact that Spain's economy was already organized for a great deal of self-sufficiency did limit somewhat the anguish that was imposed by the drastic shrinkage of Spain's access to foreign goods after 1939. Regrettably, however, that wartime experience with isolation probably also served to confirm, too long after the war, the apparent wisdom of a policy of minimizing international economic interdependence. There is some debate as to whether Spain's continuance of autarchic policies after 1945 was entirely imposed by conditions outside Spain or whether it was in some degree "chosen" as a natural extension of Spain's prewar preference.[9] Certainly, however, that question is academic, since the government's choice was uncontroversial as a result of the absence of genuinely good alternatives up until at least 1950. Postwar trade in Europe in that period was tightly regulated through bilateral trade and payments agreements, and European trade with North America after 1948 was largely dependent on Marshall Plan arrangements in which Spain did not participate.

THE REGULATED ECONOMY

The Spanish economy of the late 1940s and most of the 1950s was subject to extensive regulation and control. The regime has been described as a "corporate state," neither "uncontrolled free enterprise" nor a system with "universal public ownership of productive resources." While ownership of the means of production was largely in private hands (the chief exceptions being the enterprises that came under the sponsorship of the national holding company, INI, Instituto Nacional de Industria), the market mechanism had only a limited role in allocating resources. Official regulatory bodies deeply influenced the uses to which private property could be put.

In the agricultural sector, for example, extensive government intervention in the form of price controls and rationing had near disastrous consequences on several occasions. The ceiling price for wheat led to widespread avoidance of wheat cultivation in the 1940s when cereal output was already deficient and when foreign exchange for imports was critically scarce. A result was that the great majority of Spaniards went hungry in that decade. While the National Institute of Colonization (founded in 1939) sought improved agricultural efficiency through the planning and financing of irrigation projects and through encouraging the exchange of land parcels to consolidate geographically disparate small holdings, little was achieved along these lines before the late 1950s.

The policy of the state toward manufacturing and industry, in conjunction with the control of foreign trade, aimed at the substitution of domestic production for imports, especially in defense-related industries. Because of the Law for the Protection of Industry of 1939, no new industrial capacity could be created and no existing capacity could be modified or relocated without official approval. On the other hand, the state could offer incentives to private investors in the form of tax reductions, tariff protection, import licenses, and even guaranteed rates of return to induce investment commitments. Firms accepting incentives were usually required to purchase in Spain such intermediate goods and equipment as were officially determined to be available in Spain. Under other legislation, the state could fix prices for the output of those firms that were identified as having monopoly or near-monopoly power in the domestic market.

The creation of INI in 1941 was an approach to industrialization adopted from Italy. INI's charge was to promote enterprises especially important to Spain's national interest. It had access to borrowing at the national treasury and at the Bank of Spain and was eligible for fiscal incentives and favorable treatment in terms of international exchange rates and licenses to import raw materials. Between 1942 and 1945 INI participated in 20 enterprises and, by the time of its subsequent zenith, its enterprises generated 10 percent of Spain's gross industrial product and employed 4 percent of the labor force.[10]

Institutions engaged in banking and finance were protected up to 1959 by a "status quo" policy which banned the establishment of new banking institutions. The policy's origins went back to the efforts of Nationalist forces during the civil war to regulate a highly disrupted financial structure. The policy, which was of course highly advantageous to existing institutions, was reaffirmed in 1946. Under it, the five largest Spanish banks (Bilbao, Viscaya, Hispano-Americano, Ešpanol de Credito, and Central) were able enormously to expand their power and influence. Unlike banks in Britain and the United States, Spanish banks, of course, have traditionally played a "development" role, taking equity positions in client firms, underwriting their new securities, and then providing renewable lines of short-term credit. This role has substituted for the absence of a well-functioning competitive capital market and it has also, no doubt, inhibited the development of such a market. In the 1940s and 1950s, each large or developing Spanish firm increasingly associated itself with one of the large banks and shared with the bank its management decisions. Since government-imposed interest ceilings and credit restrictions gave the banks based in Madrid—geographically close to the authorities—some advantage over banks that were based in Bilbao and Barcelona, the general scarcity of credit helped pull the headquarters of many of the large industrial firms toward the Madrid headquarters of the favored banks. By the mid-1950s, Madrid-based banks controlled 67 percent of all Spanish bank branches and had 62 percent of all deposits. Approximately 55 percent of Spain's largest firms were, by that time, also headquartered in Madrid. It can be assumed that the rise in power of the Madrid financial institutions relative to those in the Basque country and Catalonia was not unwelcome to the Franco regime in view of the government's concerns over Basque and Catalan political independence aspirations.

Labor-management relations in the Spain of the 1940s and 1950s were regulated in a system of vertical "syndicates"—organizations which came to cover all sectors of Spanish economic activity. In general, all employees and employers (except public officials, some professionals, and domestic servants and their employers) were required to join appropriate national syndicates for their respective industries or industry groups. While employees and employers shared representation in consultative assemblies at the local and national levels of the syndicates, key syndicate officers were appointed by the government. Strikes were forbidden but so also were layoffs for economic (as distinguished from disciplinary) reasons. The syndicates were justified by the government as being a means of organizing economic activity that used negotiation, regulation, and dialogue, rather than the labor-management conflict and "anarchic competition" among firms that was said to characterize free market societies. In fact, the syndicate organizations greatly strengthened the regulatory authority of the state over industry and neutralized the potential for labor unrest.

State control over international trade and payments was an especially effective dimension through which the government guided Spanish economic activity from 1940 to 1958. Whereas Spain's protection of its domestic producers from foreign competition in the 1920s had typically taken the form of import tariffs, protectionism after 1939 was generally in the form of quantitative restrictions on trade and extensive regulation of foreign exchange transactions. Both imports and exports were licensed by country of origin or destination so that the level and composition of trade was tightly controlled. In foreign exchange, there was a single overvalued exchange rate for the peseta, accompanied by the rationing of foreign exchange supplies, from 1939 to 1948. After 1948, multiple exchange rates were used, permitting the authorities to penalize or reward traders through control of the rate at which their exchange transactions were carried out.[11] As in the rest of Europe at that time, Spain's trade was framed by bilaterally negotiated trade agreements that specified trade quotas, by commodity, for each country.

Foreign investment in Spain was discouraged by the overvaluation of the peseta and by requirements that Spanish nationals have majority ownership in all enterprises. Furthermore, there were official restraints on the degree to which both profits and principal of foreign owned capital could be repatriated.

The performance of the economy under the weight of this regulatory burden and in the context of the end of wartime profiteering and several years of devastating drought, was poor. Indeed, the national income in constant prices declined an average of nearly 1 percent per annum from its already low wartime levels in the four years, 1946-1950, according to the data of the National Economic Council. Corruption was widespread in the regulatory apparatus, and there were extensive black markets for foreign exchange and for foodstuffs. Permits for industrial expansion, establishment, or relocation were allocated without adequate attention to the relative efficiency of these capital allocations, and the protection from import competition that was afforded domestic industries stimulated import substitution at the expense of production in potentially more effective export sectors. Firms with good political connections enjoyed privileges, while less well connected firms languished in frustration. Economically entrenched firms were protected, not only from imports but also from possibly more efficient Spanish firms, as a result of the various regulations and by the connections established firms had with the protected banks and public officials. While INI helped initiate and expand numerous enterprises, its contributions to total investment were partly offset by the climate of uncertainty that it created for private investors who could not predict the moves of the privileged state holding company. It was a time when income and power gravitated toward a new political elite that coalesced out of landed traditional aristocrats, new chieftans of industry and finance, and leaders of the military—a number of whom were given leadership positions in the regulatory agencies. As happens in most countries trying to develop under state management, Spain's economy became more sharply dualized during the period, with one sector composed of the relatively large, more technologically advanced, officially favored enterprises and the other composed of small, less advanced and politically anonymous firms.

FROM OSTRACISM TO ACCEPTANCE

Politically speaking, Spain achieved a remarkable comeback from ostracism to acceptance in the space of eight years, 1945 to 1953. That it was able to do so was due partly to the reasonably clear understanding by its leaders of realistic national goals and objectives, and to their purposeful adherence to their perception of the national interest. Certainly, Spain experienced a shocking series of setbacks following the Second World War.

Perhaps Spain was more prepared to face the postwar era than those nations which had been so intent on "first, surviving, and then, winning or losing the war." Spain had managed to maintain neutrality. But while it had been helpful enough to the allied cause to avoid being placed in "enemy" status, Spain's "help" had not been enough to justify its inclusion in the Marshall Plan for the recovery of Western Europe.[12]

Three strongly negative factors placed obstacles in the path of Spain's return to respectability. First, there was the short-lived attempt at cooperation between the United States and the Soviet Union, 1945-1948, which precluded any close liaison between the United States and Spain in view of the reciprocal Spanish-Soviet hostility remaining from the fall of the Spanish Republic to Franco's forces in 1939.

Second, there was the birth of the United Nations, where countries unsympathetic to Spain had a veto in the Security Council, and this gave the international community a strong weapon to use against Spain. The veto was used with devastating effect on Spain from 1945 to 1950, and Spain was not admitted to the United Nations until 1955.

Third, there were coincidental major changes in leadership in both Great Britain and the United States which almost certainly had an adverse impact on Spain. The death of President Roosevelt and the succession of Vice President Truman to the U.S. presidency meant that leadership in America passed to a person who had not been involved in international relations during World War II. Moreover, the new president was a committed Protestant who was susceptible to the persistent complaints of the Protestant community, that their freedom to operate in Spain was harshly restricted by the Franco regime. In Great Britain, Winston Churchill was defeated in an election in July 1945 by Clement Atlee of the Labor Party, who took a much sterner and more critical attitude toward Franco than had Churchill.

In addition, Communist voices had gained considerable electoral strength in France and Italy. In October 1945, Communists gained over one-fourth of the seats in the French National Assembly, thereby obtaining considerable influence and strength in the government. In Italy, in the late 1940s, Communists were building up to the high point of their postwar strength at the polls. This meant, of course, that Spain could get no support from either of those governments.

It is not at all surprising that the Franco government decided to concentrate its efforts on the government of the United States and to build up the soon-to-be famous "Spanish Lobby." That lobby was initially headed by José Felix Lequerica, who had been foreign minister of Spain in 1944-1945. Earlier, at the beginning of the Second World War, he had also been Spanish ambassador to France. Lequerica was sent by the Franco government to the United States in 1948, but the United States government at that time refused his appointment because of his World War II record. Franco persisted, however, assigning Lequerica to Washington as "Inspector of Embassies and Legations." This position, of course, gave him considerably more latitude to lobby throughout the United States than he might have had as a diplomatic Chief of Mission because it freed him from the formal responsibilities accompanying such a post.

Subsequently, the Spanish Embassy in Washington found additional talent. In 1949 it employed attorney Charles Patrick Clark as counsel for the Division of Cultural Affairs. Then the embassy retained the services of the well-known firm of Cummings, Stanley, Truitt and Cross for general legal services. Cummings had been Attorney General of the United States and was already agent for the Dominican Republic, certainly a country that needed an effective lobbyist in Washington as much as did Franco Spain. Besides his own capabilities, Cummings had a significant asset to offer in the form of his partner, Truitt, who was son-in-law of Vice President Barkley. Clark's fee the first year he was hired, 1949, was $57,750. The next year, it was $121,000. The Cummings firm, according to Department of Justice records, received only $22,065.

The "Spanish Lobby" could be divided into four parts: (1) political, (2) military, (3) religious, and (4) business. The political lobby was headed by Clark himself, who had seen service on the staffs of various congressional committees, including service as counsel for the Committee Investigating the National Defense Program, the committee once headed by then Senator Harry Truman. Senator Patrick McCarran of Nevada, and Representatives Zablocki and O'Konski gave strong political support to the Spanish government from their key positions in the Congress.

In its military dealings, the "Spanish Lobby" concentrated on the Navy and Air Force. These services had an obvious need for bases on the southern flank of Europe, and Spain loomed as more and more attractive to them. The Spaniards were helped by an ominous train of events: (1) the Russians attempted to blockade Berlin in 1948, and (2) the Soviets acquired atomic weaponry in 1949. Indeed, it was the Navy, represented by Admiral Forrest Sherman, which in the summer of 1951 broke the log-jam and opened up serious negotiations between the United States and Spain for bases. 13

The religious aspect of the lobby was oriented toward the Roman Catholic Church, whose representatives were generally more favorably disposed toward Spain than spokesmen for other denominations. The most notable Catholic lobbyist was the Reverend Dr. Joseph F. Thorning, editor of a review called Americas and World Affairs. Father Thorning was also very active on behalf of many of the Latin American countries, most notably the Dominican Republic. In 1946, General Franco bestowed on Thorning the Grand Cross of the Order of Isabella la Católica. Beginning in 1949, a considerable amount of all the pro-Spanish material inserted in The Congressional Record could be attributed in one manner or another to Father Thorning. 14

The fourth arm of the "Spanish Lobby" was linked with U.S. business interests. Cotton producers of the South pressed especially vigorously for an enlarged entree to Spanish markets. Spanish textile mills had an insatiable need for cotton, and the commodity was easy to sell when it had the support of Export-Import Bank loans. Later, other commodity representatives got into the act. The timber producers of the South were anxious to sell railroad ties to the ailing Spanish railroads and, among manufacturing interests joining the fray, there were producers of heavy machinery for utilities, steel mills, mines, and road construction.

SPAIN AND THE UNITED STATES:
THE GROPING TOWARD UNDERSTANDING

The forgiving and forgetting that Spaniards and Americans had to do following the Second World War did not come easily. Spain had, of course, been openly pro-fascist during the early stages of the war.[15] To Franco's credit, he did not permit Hitler and Mussolini to use Spanish territory following the overthrow of the Low Countries and France in May of 1940. Franco-haters say that he did so only because the German and Italian leaders refused to pay his price. But whatever the cause, the outcome was beneficial to the Allied cause. In addition, all through World War II, Franco Spain's Hispanidad Program in Latin America had been pointedly anti-United States. Its aim was to restore Spanish hegemony in Latin America.[16] Still further, Americans condemned the Franco government for its undemocratic character and its lack of respect for what we now call human rights.

To understand the Franco Spain viewpoint, nonetheless, one must try to think like Franco did, however difficult that might be. The thought process begins with a strong and undeviating anti-Communist orientation. Franco, after fighting the Spanish Republicans from 1936 to 1939, believed that he, more than anyone else, had defended the interests of the non-Communist world against the Soviet Union. He would have liked to receive public credit for this effort. Instead, he got treatment in the American press—led by Time and the New York Times—that was hostile and derogatory. It was also Franco's view that (1) by denying use of Spanish territory to Germany and Italy, (2) by his doing nothing to prevent the full Allied operation out of Gibraltar, and (3) by his noninterference with the Allied invasion of North Africa in 1942, he actually contributed to the Allied victory in the war.

Reflection on Franco's foreign policies, both during World War II and subsequent to the war, provides evidence of his ability to pursue a view of Spanish national interest in the face of significant odds. While he had no "grand design," he was a successful pragmatist. Hindsight suggests that Franco often had a good perception of what was achievable and optimal for Spain. His government was admittedly opportunistic. Nevertheless, things were done with care with respect to timing and costs and benefits. This quality was reflected in his handling of personnel, as well as his policies.

Franco's reading of public opinion at home was also usually accurate. Having sensed what the public would tolerate, he then gave the appearance of ignoring whatever open opposition developed. An attitude of public acquiescence in Spain was of course enhanced by an overwhelming degree of war-weariness throughout the country in the

1940s and 1950s. Elena de La Souchere, a former Republican diplomat, in An Explanation of Spain, said of the period that "No one cared to begin a contest of strength."[17] And even as late as 1961, Arthur Whitaker wrote, "Among university youths, [there is] almost universal agreement that the highest priority should be accorded to affecting a national reconciliation and, as a prerequisite, burying the civil war hatchet."[18] But lest one be misled as to the degree of agreement that can be easily reached in Spain on any matter, Whitaker also wrote, "It should be remembered that in highly individualistic and chronically discontented Spain, every Spaniard is in effect a one-man opposition party."[19]

In the minds of Americans, images of Spain undoubtedly contained elements that were positive toward a rapprochement and elements that were negative. On the positive side, there was a rebirth of the view that Spain was an important part of western civilization. Spain could also be a vital part of an American relationship with Latin America. Moreover, as has been mentioned earlier, Spain had important contributions to make to the security of the United States and its allies in Western Europe. In another vein, the United States experienced, following World War II, some reaction to the radical idealistic fervor which had flowered in the 1930s as the Soviet Union and its Eastern European satellites came to be seen as the country's potential adversaries. In the process, Spain became relatively more acceptable. Even the liberal press lowered the tone of its anti-Franco rhetoric. The stage was set for the U.S.-Spanish connection.

OPENING TO THE WEST

That political leaders can and do respond to alterations in the world balance of power was never more clearly demonstrated than by what transpired in 1949 with respect to Spain. National security became the paramount objective of American diplomacy. The Communist menace seemed threatening on all sides and even within. Mao was about to complete the takeover of mainland China. Greece was a major target of the USSR, and the United States had responded with the Truman Plan. In Latin America, military dictators were leading a new wave of repression and, thus, opening the doors to radicalism and future Communist penetration. At home, fingers were being pointed at alleged Communists and fellow-travelers. Spain took on importance as a bulwark against the spread of Communism.

In 1949, the political arm of the "Spanish Lobby" began to be heard in the Congress. The lobby found a "cause" when the United States abstained in a United Nations General Assembly vote on a resolution which would have left to the member states "full freedom of action as regards their diplomatic relations with Spain," thereby opening the possibility of restoring normal relations with that country. Secretary Acheson personally undertook to clarify the United States' position on this issue, but his explanation seemed only to provoke a more heated reaction in the Congress on the part of Spain's supporters. The flavor of the arguments on behalf of Spain, and the stridency of the lobby, are illustrated by the following selections from a statement by Senator Pat McCarran of Nevada:

> MR. McCARRAN. Mr. President, if it is stated that the Spanish Government does not recognize religious freedom in Spain, that statement is false propaganda.
>
> . . .
>
> I have this thought in mind. I wonder why any democratic nation, any God-fearing democratic people, and no one will deny that the people of Spain have been such all down through the ages, should be denied the right to receive the benefits of ECA which we are extending to other nations of Europe. . . .
>
> . . .
>
> However, I believe that anyone who is a strategist will agree that there is nothing more essential to the military success of the North Atlantic Pact—if it means military success—than the Iberian Peninsula.
>
> . . .
>
> The Secretary of State volunteered the statement that it is commonly known that Spain is a Fascist Government. I drew his attention to the fact that we had full diplomatic relations with Czechoslovakia, Yugoslavia and other satellite countries and, indeed, with Moscow. All those nations have out-and-out and openly communistic forms of government. Shall we say, Mr. Secretary of State, that we will deny recognition to a democratic form of government while at the same time recognizing communism by sending our representatives of the highest echelon into diplomatic relations with communistic governments?
>
> . . .
>
> I do not care whether some wag or some other person or some official calls the form of government of Spain a Fascist form of government. I have grave doubt whether any person would have authority to make such a statement, or whether facts can be demonstrated in support of such a matter. [20]

Still, there was a powerful opposition to Spain in the United States. Concomitant with the 1949 discussions in the U.N. General Assembly regarding Spain, the Senate Foreign Relations Committee was holding hearings on the North Atlantic Treaty Organization (NATO). The two most stalwart members of that committee, Senator Tom Connally of Texas, Chairman, and Senator Vandenberg, ranking Republican member of the committee, made public their views that Spain was not desired in NATO nor was there any foreseeable possibility of its admission. [21]

Time and events, however, were on the Spanish side. From a political standpoint, the opposition to Spain of Secretary Acheson and his State Department colleagues was becoming more and more difficult to defend. The loss to the Communists of mainland China made the State Department an easy target for the foes of its policies. In fact, the groundwork was being laid for the era associated with the questionable accusations and allegations of Senator Joseph McCarthy. The friends of Spain were not easily dissuaded. In the Senate Appropriations Committee they were able to include an amendment to a European Recovery Program bill (despite the fact that there was no substantive mention of Spain during the hearings) which would have earmarked fifty million dollars of the funds available to the European Cooperation Administration for assistance to Spain. While the amendment was adopted in the committee, it eventually was defeated on the floor after vigorous debate. [22]

National security factors began to weigh more and more in favor of Spain. This became clear in May of 1950 with the preparation of a Spanish policy paper that was co-authored by William Dunham, Spanish Desk Officer in the Department of State, and James Wilson of the Office of International Security Affairs in the Department of Defense. This paper reached the following conclusion:

> In the light of the intensification of the "cold war," the potential military importance of Spain . . . [has] increased in importance to such a degree that the security interests of the U.S. and the NATO nations now require that a program . . . should be put into effect, despite political objections, in order to provide at least for indirect Spanish cooperation within the Western European strategic pattern. [23]

It is interesting to note that not until December 1950, six months after it was prepared, was the Dunham-Wilson paper forwarded by the Departments of State and Defense to the National Security Council. Heavyweights in the Pentagon were beginning to throw their support toward Spain, but there were some reservations. The top military echelon in the Air Force finally was responsible for bringing that service into line. Its civilian head, Secretary Finletter, on the other hand, happened to be one of the staunch opponents of Franco Spain. Finletter, in retrospect, had good reasons for his reservations about the military value of a pact, for he was known to have doubts that the United States would be able to use the Spanish bases unreservedly.

By the end of the year, 1950, even President Truman had relented in his opposition to doing business with the Franco government. On December 27, 1950, the President appointed movie executive Stanton Griffis as the American ambassador to Spain, ending the four-year interregnum during which the United States had been without a diplomatic chief of mission in Madrid. It should be emphasized, however, that U.S. relations with Spain had continued, simply at a lower level. The senior American diplomat during this period, with the title of Chargé d'Affaires, was Paul Culbertson. At diplomatic affairs in Spain, he ranked after all the ambassadors and ministers of fully accredited missions to the Franco government. His dispatches to Washington, nevertheless, carried as much weight as if he had been designated ambassador.

The tempo of U.S.-Spanish relations quickened in 1951. It seemed that every major international event caused Spain's stock to rise. As for relations between the United States and the Eastern European bloc headed by the Soviet Union, the cold war was now blowing strong. There was no let-up in sight in the Korean War, and the U.S. economy had to revert to a wartime basis.[24] Spain looked more and more attractive to the United States. Spain had already-tested manpower to support the defense of the West, as well as highly-valued mineral resources, notably tungsten used to harden steel. Military experts regarded the Spanish territory as a valued redoubt in support of democratic forces in Western Europe. However, as will be discussed further below, this Spanish asset of being "behind the Pyrenees" was considered by some Europeans as being hardly to their advantage.

The State Department's changing attitude toward Spain was clearly reflected in the testimony of Secretary of State Acheson before the Senate Foreign Relations Committee in February 1951:

> The importance of the association of Spain in the defense of Western Europe I think is clear. I think it is also clear that the relations of this country, and I hope of the other countries, with Spain are now entering a new phase. . . .[25]

Then in June, President Truman, who by this time was virtually the lone anti-Spanish voice in his entire administration, approved a

National Security Council (NSC) position on U.S. policy toward Spain. This, in effect, authorized efforts to seek agreement from the Spanish government for certain base facilities in that country. The NSC position evolved from the Dunham-Wilson policy paper referred to above.

Only a month later, President Truman authorized the Chief of Naval Operations, Admiral Forrest Sherman, to proceed to Spain for direct discussions with Franco. The president bluntly told the admiral, "I don't like Franco and I never will, but I won't let my personal feeling override the convictions of you military men."[26] On July 16, Admiral Sherman, Ambassador Stanton Griffis, and Lt. Commander John Fitzpatrick, USN, Assistant Naval Attache, American Embassy Madrid, met with Franco in Pardo Palace near Madrid. Fitzpatrick, by fortunate coincidence, was Admiral Sherman's son-in-law and accompanied the two principals for the purpose of taking notes. Actually, very little was placed in the written record. According to Fitzpatrick, "They talked about the need to improve U.S.-Spanish relations in view of world conditions, and they agreed, They left the question of bases and military or economic aid to later negotiations."[27]

Now that the roadblocks had been removed, the United States government went ahead to publicize the importance of its new relationship with the Franco government. The following press statement of Secretary Acheson, dated July 18, 1951, is illuminating:

Admiral Sherman's interview with General Franco on Monday has caused widespread speculation in the press both here and abroad. The facts are as follows:

Military authorities are in general agreement that Spain is of strategic importance to the general defense of Western Europe. As a natural corollary to this generally accepted conclusion, tentative and exploratory conversations have been undertaken with the Spanish Government with the sole purpose of ascertaining what Spain might be willing and able to do which would contribute to the strengthening of the common defense against possible aggression.

We have been talking with the British and French Governments for many months about the possible role of Spain in relation to the general defense of Western Europe. We have not been able to find a common position on this subject with these Governments for reasons of which we are aware and understand. However, for the strategic reasons outlined above, the United States has initiated these exploratory conversations.

Any understanding which may ultimately be reached

will supplement our basic policy of building the defensive strength of the West. It has been and is our firm intention to see to it that if Western Europe is attacked it will be defended—and not liberated. The presence of American armed forces in Western Europe bears witness to this intent as does the appointment, at the request of our NATO allies, of General Eisenhower as Supreme Commander.

We are sending vast amounts of military and other aid to these allies for whom a clear priority has been established. There will be no change in this procedure. In other words, the North Atlantic Treaty is fundamental to our policy in Europe, and the closest possible cooperation with our NATO allies will remain the keystone of this policy. [28]

In this way the Secretary of State sought to reassure America's Western European allies that the emerging Spanish connection did not represent any downgrading of the primacy of the NATO alliance and especially that it did not represent any easy willingness to retreat to a shelter "behind the Pyrenees."

Following the high drama of Admiral Sherman's visit to Spain, the hard work of detailed negotiations began. Franco had agreed that American economic and military survey teams could come to Spain. In late August 1951, a military mission, headed by Air Force Major General James W. Spry, which also included Army and Navy officers, went to Spain. It made its report at the end of October, concluding that, while Spanish bases did have strategic value, they might have questionable value in wartime because of the Franco requirement that Spain maintain full sovereignty over the bases.

The economic mission to Spain was headed by Dr. Sidney Sufrin, Syracuse University, who represented the Economic Cooperation Administration, and included Export-Import Bank officials. Their report, concluded in November 1951, reportedly said that the Spanish economy was "being held together by bailing wire and hope." [29]

Admiral Sherman, who was assigned the lead role as this act of the U.S.-Spanish drama unfolded, played his part well but made only one appearance. In a tragic irony of history, Sherman died of a heart attack in Naples, only six days after he met Franco in Madrid.

SPAIN'S ECONOMIC CRISIS, 1949-1951

Spain's opening to the West coincided with its production and balance of payments crisis of 1949-1950. The immediate cause of the production failure in Spain was severe drought. The years 1948, 1949, and 1950 were all years of low rainfall, and by the summer of 1950, Spain's too few reservoirs were filled to no more than 10 percent of their capacity. The index of agricultural production for this three years averaged only 78.4 (1953-55 = 100) as compared to 98.4 for the other seven years of the 1946-55 decade. Furthermore, the empty reservoirs forced a reduction in electricity output that closed many factories, especially in Catalonia. Registered unemployment increased by 43 percent between 1947 and 1950, and critical exports, such as textiles and publications, buffeted by recession in North America as well as by power shortages at home, declined. After Franco required employers to pay their employees whether they worked or not, and after the state enlarged social welfare expenditures, inflation accelerated from 6.5 percent in 1949 to 18 percent in 1950, and then to almost 30 percent in 1951. Selected peseta exchange rates were repeatedly devalued in 1949 and 1950, with a view to restoring or sustaining investment and tourism in Spain and discouraging less essential imports. But farmers withheld their crops from the Wheat Institute to protest unrealistically low official grain prices and, then in January 1950, both Argentina and Brazil, facing balance of payments difficulties of their own, suspended further credits to Spain. Hunger demonstrations were organized in Madrid and, at the beginning of 1950, Spain's Ministry of Industry and Commerce appealed for "any country whatsoever" to ship grain to the Spanish people.[30]

Critical help came from the United States in early 1950 in the form of loans from two private banks. While in both cases the banks required that a significant margin of gold collateral be deposited before the loans were disbursed, on February 8, Chase Manhattan Bank approved a loan to the Spanish government of $25 million and on March 24, the National City Bank of New York approved a $20 million credit.

In February-March 1950, the first postwar assistance to Spain from the U.S. government came in the form of sales of potatoes from U.S. surplus stocks. On February 15, the Spanish government announced in Washington its purchase of 1.1 million pounds of potatoes at one cent per 100 pounds and then, in March, it bought no less than 85 million pounds at the same price. By the end of March, Spanish potato rationing ended.[31]

While Spanish efforts to obtain U.S. government credits failed in 1949, in 1950 they at last became possible. Only weeks after the Communist invasion of South Korea, the U.S. Senate accepted, in August 1950, a proposal by Senator Pat McCarran to authorize the Export-Import Bank to lend Spain $100 million, the loan to be administered by the Economic Cooperation Administration outside the

Marshall Plan. In conference committee, the authorization was cut from $100 million to $62.5 million and, in that form, it passed both houses of Congress on August 28 and obtained the presidential signature. The U.S. measure required Spain to prepare a recovery plan just as Marshall Plan countries had been required to do—and a Spanish plan was approved by Washington early in 1951. In February 1951, the first loans under the $62.5 million McCarran authorization were made—credits totaling $12.5 million to be used for the purchase of cotton, fertilizer, tractors, and equipment for a new fertilizer plant.

For a time during 1951 tungsten again became an issue between Spain and the United States and posed some threat to the thawing of relations between the two countries. The problem arose because the demand for Spanish tungsten intensified with the beginning of the Korean War and resulted in sharp price rises. The price of Spanish tungsten delivered in the United States rose from $2,300 a ton in late 1950 to $4,740 in 1951. In response to the change in demand, Spanish production rose from 819 tons in 1949 to 1,864 in 1951. But when Spanish producers then demanded a minimum price (f.o.b. Spain) of $4,970 at about the same time that the price of Spanish mercury— also in short supply—rose from $55 per standard flask to $200, frustration and anger were voiced in the U.S. Congress.

Such incidents were, however, on a longer view, mere friction, and U.S. loans to Spain continued. Three credits announced under the Export-Import Bank program in the spring and summer of 1951 totaled $23.65 million and were used for the purchase of wheat, coal, equipment and services for the Spanish Railways, and in the development of mineral production and hydroelectric power. In October 1951, the Congress voted Spain a further $100 million.

EASING OF "QUARANTINE"

The United Nations finally lifted its ban on diplomatic relations with Spain and on Spanish participation in the U.N. agencies in 1950. As early as May 1949, the General Assembly's Political and Security Committee voted to let U.N. members resume full diplomatic relations with Spain, but this action did not receive confirmation from the General Assembly itself. Nevertheless, early in 1950, Colombia exchanged ambassadors with Spain, and Korea extended recognition. Finally, on November 4, 1950, the General Assembly repealed its 1946 diplomatic boycott by a vote of 38-10, with 12 abstentions. It endorsed U.N. member assignment of diplomatic representation to Spain and opened the door to Spanish membership in those U.N. specialized agencies that admitted non-U.N. members.[32]

Spain was not slow in capitalizing on its admissibility to U.N. agencies. In the spring of 1951, it sought and obtained membership in the Food and Agricultural Organization, the World Health Organization, and the International Civil Aviation Organization. In November 1952, it was elected to membership in UNESCO and in December to the International Telecommunications Union.

Spanish economic recovery from the crisis of the late 1940s coincided with the changes in its foreign relations, led by its new U.S. connection. In mid-summer, 1951, rain began to fall on the peninsula and, by autumn, Spanish reservoirs were two-thirds full. Potato production doubled in the year, dried druit and olive production trebled, and output of tomatoes, cotton, and tobacco increased by percentages ranging from 12 to 40 percent. Industrial production responded to expanding demand and renewed availability of energy and materials. High export prices for tungsten and mercury helped the balance of payments, as did economic recovery in France, Britain, and Central Europe. Spain recorded its first postwar balance of trade surplus in 1951, and, in 1952, the government paid off, eight and one-half years ahead of schedule, the balance of a $50 million long-term debt to the International Telephone and Telegraph Company that had been incurred in 1945 as a result of Spanish nationalization of telecommunications facilities.

It is not possible clearly to identify the contribution of U.S. assistance to Spain's 17.6 percent spurt of growth in real national income in 1951, but it was, without doubt, significant. U.S. Export-Import Bank loans approved between September 6, 1950, and August 31, 1951, taken alone, came to $45.8 million. To put this amount in perspective, one can note that it equaled 9.5 percent of Spain's 1951 exports of merchandise of $482 million. The $4.1 million in U.S. loans for development of electric power stations was 13.5 percent of the estimated annual average Spanish investment in such stations, 1947-51.[33] The $6.7 million provided between September 1950 and August 1951 for steel and fertilizer plants was of the order of 35 percent of the total capital raised by fifteen representative Spanish steel companies over the entire five-year, 1947-51, period.[34] Similarly, the $7.5 million provided the Spanish State Railways (RENFE) was apparently an important input. It amounted to 33 percent of the 900 million pesetas of annual debt issue allowed RENFE in the government's General Plan of Reconstruction for that year. All of these ratios, then, suggest that the U.S. contribution was quite significant.

A spurt of monetary growth (to 12.6 percent), together with real output expansion and increased expenditures abroad by the Spanish government on modernization of military equipment, caused the Spanish balance of trade seriously to deteriorate in 1952. Real output continued to grow in that year—although at a 4.7 percent rate rather than the extraordinary 17.6 percent burst of 1951. In per capita terms, output in Spain reached pre-civil war levels for the first time in 1952.

THE MILITARY BASE NEGOTIATIONS, 1952-1953

Washington needed a few months to digest the reports of the military mission to Spain, headed by Major General Spry, and the economic mission to Spain, headed by Sidney Sufrin, whose reports were submitted in the early fall of 1951. Unfortunately, the year 1952 did not begin ostentatiously for U.S.-Spanish relations. Ambassador Stanton Griffis resigned his position in late January, saying that the future of the relationship depended on the Department of Defense.[35] President Truman, who had already eaten considerable crow, was giving ground grudgingly. On February 7, 1952, he stated in a press conference he was "not very fond" of Spain under its present government.[36] While the president did not seriously undercut his own policy, such statements by him did make it easier for the footdraggers in the government to move slowly.

Secretary Acheson was by now convinced of the value of the Spanish bases, and he began to move. He is credited with three significant appointments. First, Ambassador Lincoln McVeigh, formerly ambassador to Portugal and Greece, was named Chief of Mission in Madrid. Second, Air Force Major General August W. Kissner was chosen to head up the military negotiations. His team would include Navy and Army officers, as well as those from his own service. Third, George Train, of the Mutual Security Administration, who had been with Ambassador McVeigh in the negotiations for bases while in Portugal, was named head of the Economic Negotiating Mission.

The formal negotiations actually began with the arrival of General Kissner in April 1952. The heads of the two negotiating teams were the Spanish Foreign Minister Martin Artajo, and Ambassador McVeigh, but they came into the negotiations only at crucial points. Most of the work was carried out by General Kissner, on the military side, who dealt directly with General Jorge Vigon, Director General of the Spanish High General Staff. Mr. Train conducted his negotiations with the Minister of Commerce, Manuel Arburua, an experienced international banker who had been president of the Banco Exterior of Spain before his appointment to the cabinet by General Franco the preceding year.

The negotiations were prolonged and difficult, lasting approximately sixteen months.[37] On the Spanish side, Franco, even though not physically involved, was the brooding presence. Having overcome

Spain's ostracism by the U.N., the long break in relations with the United States, and even the open dislike of his government by Secretary Acheson and President Truman, Franco now was not unwilling to put the Americans in their place. He had regained international acceptance for Spain. Next he wanted an agreement with the United States on terms acceptable to him. His three major objectives were:

- First, to obtain substantial military assistance in the form of equipment to update Spanish forces with modern material
- Second, to obtain as much economic assistance as he could extract from the United States
- Third, to retain Spanish sovereignty over the bases, including use of the Spanish flag, and to insure that there were restrictions on the United States' use of them

As will be seen below, he achieved his goal with point number three, and he probably got as much as he could have hoped for in points one and two. One must recall that Franco's bargaining power had limits. He pressed the limits, nonetheless.

OPPOSITION WITHIN SPAIN

Although Franco had made up his own mind to negotiate with the United States for his objectives in return for bases, he did not have a green light from his fellow countrymen. The main opposition to the bases inside Spain came from within groups that were nominal supporters of Franco, reflecting in some degree the fact that Franco's traditional enemies were either unable to voice their opposition due to tight censorship or that they were outside of Spain. According to Whitaker, these were the groups that were the most outspoken doubters: "Nationalists were offended by the concession of bases to a foreign power and the presence of foreign troops on Spanish soil; traditionalists, by the formation of a quasi-alliance which, they alleged, violated Spain's settled policy of neutrality and isolation; and Catholics, by concessions to, and contacts with, Protestantism implicit in the proposed relationship with the United States."[38]

Franco's authority was so complete and unchallengeable, nevertheless, that he had no serious problem with the nationalists and traditionalists. Some of the more serious critics within these groups were military officers. The older ones among them were quieted by being granted early retirement at full pay. The younger ones had no choice but to respond to military discipline and accede to Franco's desires.

The Church was the principal problem. Franco had to take this group seriously. Opposition to the understanding with the United States was led by Spain's ranking prelate, Cardinal Segura, of Sevilla, who openly protested against bartering the "Catholic conscience" of Spain for "heretical dollars."[39]

THE VATICAN FIRST, THEN WASHINGTON

At this point Franco showed his shrewdness. He wanted to build a tri-partite alliance which would link the Vatican, Washington, and Madrid.[40] The Concordat of 1851, which had long determined Spain's relations with the Vatican, had been abrogated in 1931, with the advent of the Republican Socialist government of Spain. The moral support that a new agreement with the Vatican would bring about would ease some of the criticism of the Franco regime while giving it a positive force throughout the Roman Catholic world. Consequently, as early as 1951, Franco sent as Ambassador to the Vatican one of his most respected advisors, Joaquin Ruiz-Gimenez. The latter spoke directly to Pope Pius XII regarding the possibility of a new Concordat, and delivered a personal letter from Franco to the Pope. Negotiations formally began in January 1952 when Franco appointed a new Vatican Ambassador, Fernando Maria de Castiella.

At this time Madrid was in any case the site of an important political discussion relating to the Spanish Church. Education had long been a source of conflict between church leaders and the Franco government. Under the Spanish system, high school education, practically speaking, was not available to the children of the poor. To make matters worse, 95 percent of the population could not afford to send their children to the state-operated colleges and universities. The result was that in 1952-1953, 15 percent of the adult population over ten years of age was illiterate, leaving a "small almost self-perpetuating group of college-educated individuals [who] tended to dominate business, industry and the higher echelons of the government."[41]

Protracted negotiations between Spanish church officials and the Minister of Education, Joaquin Ruiz-Gimenez, who had initiated the talks with the Vatican on the new Concordat in 1951, finally resulted, in July 1952, in an agreement concerning economic matters, curricular design, and control of Spanish education. The Vatican approved the high school reform system, and, in turn, on February 25, 1953, the Cortes passed the necessary reform legislation. The agreement on education opened the doors to the new Concordat. The Spanish Foreign Minister, Martin Artajo, shifted his priority from Washington to Rome, where he conducted quiet talks with Pius XII.

According to most observers, the Concordat simply recognized the return of Franco Spain to the fold of the Roman Catholic Church. According to the papal newspaper, l'Osservatore Romano, "Spain reaffirms those principles which form the basis of the prosperity of the family and the nation: full recognition of religious marriage, the Christian education of youth, and freedom for the Church to carry out the apostolate. The Holy See . . . confirms—with the adaptations required by the contingencies of the present day—the traditional privileges that have been conceded to Spain in the course of centuries. "[42]

It should be noted that the agreement with the Vatican was signed exactly one month before the Pact of Madrid with the United States. The Vatican accord made it easier for Franco to proceed with the final stages of the U.S. negotiations because it helped to silence church opposition in Spain to the base agreements. On hindsight it is interesting to note that the Roman Catholic leaders in Spain were no more successful than the Protestant leaders had been in the United States in stopping the movement of the two governments toward accommodation of mutually perceived national interests. The pragmatic considerations of security and economics overruled church opposition in both countries to the Pact of Madrid.

The U.S.-Spanish agreements, coupled with the Vatican Concordat, were described at the time as a major victory for Franco. Herbert L. Matthews, writing in the New York Times, made this comment on the events of 1953: "It was the high spot of Franco's post-war career. He had defeated his enemies in and out of Spain, he had refused to yield one inch to liberalism; and now his efforts had gained the highest sanction from two of the highest powers of the world, religious and secular—the Vatican and the United States. "[43]

CHANGING THE GUARD IN WASHINGTON

By the time Dwight Eisenhower was elected president of the United States, the American public had been conditioned for the base agreements with Spain, even though the negotiations had not been completed. However, the pace of the negotiations slowed for the first few months of 1953. On the Spanish side, as explained above, this was probably due to the priority that the Franco government gave to negotiating the Concordat with the Vatican. On the American side, several months were required for the members of the new administration to get in harness.

President Eisenhower, with his vast experience in Europe, never questioned the agreements. As much as any other American, he knew their potential value. Secretary Dulles knew Spain from his many years as head of the New York law firm Sullivan and Cromwell.

In addition Dulles had been the U.S. negotiator for the U.S.-Japanese Peace Treaty, following World War II, and he was fully aware of the strategic importance of the Spanish bases.

Ambassador McVeigh was replaced by Ambassador James Clement Dunn. Dunn was a career diplomat whose experience uniquely qualified him for the role as ambassador in Madrid. Following many years of increasingly responsible posts in the Department of State in Washington, Dunn had been assigned to the ambassadorship in Italy immediately after World War II. Thus, he was experienced in administering a substantial U.S. assistance program. His colleagues also give him credit for having helped abort the Communist thrust to win the 1948 elections in Italy. From Rome, Ambassador Dunn was transferred to Paris. In that European capital, he administered the closing phase of the Marshall Plan for another war-devastated country. From almost any standpoint, Ambassador Dunn was ideally suited for the Madrid post.

The chief negotiators for the Military Base Agreement and for the Economic Assistance Agreement, respectively, Major General August Kissner, U.S. Air Force, and George Train, remained on the country team, [44] now headed by Ambassador Dunn, until the agreements were signed on September 26, 1953.

A BALANCED EQUATION

The new U.S.-Spanish connection was a balanced equation good for both sides. Spain regained international respectability and "a place in the sun;" the United States got another circle of bases in Southwestern Europe, just beyond the periphery of NATO. Whether the Spaniards realized it or not, and had they realized it they might not have liked it, the United States had approached Spain with its traditional "sense of mission."

Americans had an awareness of the meaning of the Spanish Civil War—its "glory" for cause, its brutality, and its destructive cost. The great-grandparents and grandparents of those Americans who fought in the Second World War had told their progeny the meaning of civil war. So when thousands of World War II veterans came to Spain to man new U.S. bases, they were sympathetic to a nation which had suffered so much. They didn't have to take sides. They didn't deal with Franco. They could relate to the Spanish people intellectually and emotionally.

Those same Americans were also visible symbols of freedom. Even though they followed instructions to maintain low visibility, including the wearing of civilian clothes when off duty, there was no way their characteristic openness could be bottled up. The Americans brought their freedom with them, along with their humor, and the Spaniards vicariously participated in the former of these and enthusiastically joined the latter.

The most obvious part of the international relationship was the increase in security that each nation offered the other. The United States was not prepared to pay whatever price might have been demanded for the agreement. Had Spain overreached, their counterparts would have walked away from the table. Rubottom learned this from his briefings before he went to Spain in June 1953, and he heard it again in recent discussions with several well-placed sources, including Dean Rusk, who was Assistant Secretary of State under Secretaries Marshall and Acheson and later himself Secretary of State.

It bears some repeating that Spain had no other partner in sight. The nation could have tightened its belt some more, but economic unrest was so widespread in 1951, starting in Barcelona and then spreading to Madrid, that Franco, himself, saw fit to make concessions to the workers. On the other hand, the United States wanted and needed the bases in Spain. That need, and nothing else, finally brought a reluctant President Truman to accept the prospect of an agreement with Franco Spain. The pact was an illustration of the exploitation of intersecting national interests.

NOTES

1. Salvador Madriaga, Spain—A Modern History (New York: Praeger, 1958), p. 273.

2. New York Times, September 28, 1953.

3. New York Herald Tribune, July 28, 1951.

4. Arthur P. Whitaker, Spain and Defense of the West (New York: Harper & Brothers, 1961), p. 92.

5. Commissioner for Economic and Social Development Planning, Presidency of the Government of Spain, Economic and Social Development Program for Spain, 1964-1967 (Baltimore: The Johns Hopkins University Press, 1965), p. 9. It might be noted, however, that housing losses in Spain may have amounted to only 0.5 percent of the total housing stock, whereas in France, during the Second World War, the loss may have been 4.0 percent, and in Germany 24.0 percent. Semanas Social de España (Burgos, 1945), cited in Joseph Harrison, An Economic History of Modern Spain (New York: Holmes and Maier, 1978), p. 153.

6. See Harrison, An Economic History of Modern Spain, p. 145. Even in power, the Nationalists, too, were burdened with civil war debts and achieved settlement on some only through price concessions on tungsten sales to Germany during the Second World War.

7. J. Lee Schneidman, ed., Spain and Franco, 1949-59 (New York: Facts on File, 1973), pp. 25-28.

8. The United States joined other governments in complying with this resolution.

9. See Luis Gamir, "El periodo 1939-1959: La autarquia y la política de estabilización," in L. Gamir (ed.), Política Económica de España, vol. 1 (Introduction. Instrumentos), 4th ed. (Madrid: Alianza Universidad. Textos, 1980), pp. 45-70.

10. By 1975 INI had become sole owner of 16 enterprises, was an equity participant in 59, and had a role in 200 more. It was the dominant factor in several heavy industries, including shipbuilding, steel, and aluminum, and it was an important force in others, such as petroleum refining, automobile manufacturing, aircraft manufacture, air transport, chemicals, and tourism.

11. There were, for example, in 1948, nine rates, varying from 11.22 to 27.38 pesetas per dollar, at which authorities might sell exchange to importers, and there were fifteen rates, from 10.95 to 21.90 pesetas per dollar, at which they might buy exchange from exporters. Rates were applied to classes of imports, exports, and service and investment transactions, and, by determining the rate applicable to a type of transaction, the authorities could implicitly tax or subsidize that class of transactions.

12. Willard Beaulac, Counselor of Embassy in the American Embassy, Madrid, during World War II, wrote in his book Career Ambassador, "It is doubtful . . . that the American public ever realized how important to the success of our military plans were a neutral Spain and a Gibraltar in Allied hands." (New York: Macmillan, 1951), p. 176.

13. The Air Force, nonetheless, was designated as the lead service when the JUSMAAG (Joint U.S. Military Assistance and Advisory Group) was established in Spain in 1953.

14. Brent Scowcroft, Congress and Foreign Policy: An Examination of Congressional Attitudes Toward the Foreign Aid Programs to Spain and Yugoslavia (unpublished Ph.D. dissertation, Columbia University, 1967), p. 31.

15. A knowledgeable and respected source for evidence of Franco's support of the Axis powers is Emmet John Hughes, Report from Spain (New York: Holt, 1947).

16. Rubottom, who served in the Office of Naval Intelligence during World War II, remembers the strong anti-American thrust of the Franco propagandists, especially in Paraguay, where he was assigned in the last year of World War II.

17. Rubottom lived in Madrid from 1953 to 1956. One of his hunting companions and close friends said, "I am anti-Franco, but Spain needs no more war. Time is on our side. We shall outlast him."

18. Whitaker, Spain and Defense of the West, p. 194.

19. Ibid., p. 156.

20. U.S., Congressional Record, 81st Cong., 1 Sess., 1949, XCV, Part 5, pp. 5965-67.

21. New York Times, May 13, 1949.

22. In 1948, Representative O'Konski also had tried without success to include funds for Spain in the House appropriations bill of the European Recovery Program.

23. The classification of this paper was downgraded, under the Freedom of Information Act, at the request of Stanley Byron Weeks, for use in his unpublished doctoral dissertation, U.S. Defense Policy towards Spain, 1950-1976, American University, Washington, D.C.

24. Rubottom, on duty in the Department of State, participated in the June 1951 meeting of Foreign Ministers of the Western Hemisphere where the work of the Economic Committee was aimed at insuring that the United States had access to essential minerals and other commodities from Latin America.

25. U.S. Congress, Senate, Committee on Foreign Relations, Committee on Armed Services, Assignment of Ground Forces of the United States to Duty in the European Area, Hearings, 82nd Congress, 1st Session, 1951, p. 87.

26. Benjamin Welles, Spain, The Gentle Anarchy (New York: Praeger, 1965), p. 287.

27. Ibid.

28. Scowcroft, Congress and Foreign Policy, p. 76.

29. New York Times, October 28, 1951.

30. Schneidman, ed., Spain and Franco, p. 49.

31. Ibid., p. 49.

32. Ibid., p. 55.

33. This percentage is based on estimated investment of 6,000 million pesetas in the entire 1947-1951 quinquinium given in Banco Urquijo, Servicios de Estudios, La Economía Española y La Reconstrucción, 1947-1951, Madrid, 1952, p. 26. The exchange rate employed for this and other dollar-peseta comparisons for 1951 was 39.577 pesetas to the dollar, the average 1951 "free market" rate.

34. This percentage is based on a Banco Urquijo estimate of 750 million pesetas as the total equity and debt capital raised, 1947-1951, by 15 representative Spanish steel companies. Banco Urquijo, Servicios de Estudios, La Economía y La Reconstrucción 1947-1951, Madrid, 1952, p. 38.

35. New York Times, January 22, 1952, p. 14.

36. Ibid., February 8, 1952, p. 1.

37. One might note that the Panama Canal Treaty negotiations between the United States and Panama ending in 1977 lasted for a full decade and were carried out in two phases with several top negotiators on each side.

38. Whitaker, Spain and Defense of the West, p. 41.

39. Ibid.

40. Jose Mario Armero, The Foreign Policy of Franco (Barcelona: Editoria Planeta, 1978), p. 162.

41. Schneidman, Spain and Franco, p. 91.

42. Ibid., p. 93.

43. Ibid., p. 105.

44. The term "country team" came into usage during the days of the Marshall Plan. Its three principal members were the ambassador, the head of the military mission, and the head of the economic or "operations" mission. Other senior members of the U.S. government staff were added to the team as required. Since the end of the major U.S. assistance programs, "country team" has remained as the designation of the group responsible for carrying out U.S. foreign policy at a foreign post, that is, the chief of diplomatic mission and his principal advisors.

2

The "Connection"
Is Turned on

On September 26, 1953, a new era began in U.S.-Spanish
relations. The leadership of both nations had resolved their doubts
and committed themselves to an agreement of indefinite duration.
The basic defense agreement was for two successive periods of five
years each unless a termination procedure was placed in effect. To
terminate, either of the two governments could notify the other of its
intention to end the agreement, thereby beginning a consultation
period of six months; if no concurrence were reached during that
time, the agreement would terminate one year after the conclusion
of the period of consultation. Thus, the agreement could be as short
as six and one-half years, or as long as eleven and one-half years.

The three separate but linked agreements, on defense, economic
aid, and mutual defense assistance, came to be known as the Pact of
Madrid. As executive agreements, they took effect immediately since,
for the U.S. side, Senate ratification was not required, and for the
Spanish side, their submission for approval to the Franco-controlled
Cortes was simply pro forma. By the process of elimination the
authors of this study decided to call the new relationship a "connection." The arrangement was not a treaty, in contrast with the North
Atlantic Treaty Organization (NATO), and the Inter-American Defense
Treaty, known as the Rio Treaty. Neither was there an "alliance,"
due to the vagueness of the commitment made by each party to the
other. Both parties agreed, however, that it was a practical accord,
a useful "connection." It opened the door for Spain's re-entry to the
family of Western nations and was an alternative to Spain's participation in NATO.

The basic Defense Agreement consisted of a preamble and five
articles. The tone of the text was set in its first clause, "Faced with

31

the danger that threatens the Western world . . . ." The United States
committed itself to provide military assistance to Spain for a period
of "several years" and, in return, received the right "subject to
terms and conditions to be agreed," "to develop, maintain and utilize
for military purposes, jointly with the Government of Spain . . .
areas and facilities in territory under Spanish jurisdiction . . . ."
These areas remained "under Spanish flag and command," and "the
time and manner of wartime utilization of said areas and facilities"
would be "as mutually agreed upon." The kind of consultation understood in the clause just quoted was covered in a secret note signed
by Ambassador Dunn and Foreign Minister Martin Artajo on the same
day as the agreement.[1] Critics in today's Spain have pointed to the
secret note as evidence of duplicity on the part of both governments.
In retrospect, however, one wonders why the note was given such
classification rather than simply being included in the text of the
agreement itself. In any event, the note was abrogated in 1970, according to Spain's former ambassador to the United States, Antonio
Garrigues.[2]

The Economic Aid Agreement committed the United States to
providing assistance only until June 30, 1956—that is, three years.
This was further evidence that the "connection" was simply an opening on which future relationships would be built, if both parties so
desired. The Mutual Defense Assistance Agreement was of indefinite
duration. Both of the assistance agreements linked the Pact of Madrid
to the U.S. Mutual Security Act of 1951, and both included extraordinary clauses referring to the United Nations Charter. The economic agreement committed the Spanish government to the proposition that "individual liberty, free institutions, and genuine independence in all countries, as well as defense against aggression, rest
largely on the establishment of a sound economy."

The Economic Aid Agreement consisted of a preamble and ten
articles, spelling out some relationships in detail. In the General
Undertakings Article, the Spanish government boldly agreed to
"stabilize its currency, establish or maintain a valid rate of exchange,
balance its government budget as soon as practicable, create or maintain internal financial stability, and generally restore or maintain
confidence in its monetary system . . . ."

Even more remarkable, considering the autarchic economy
which characterized Spain at this time, that country also agreed to
"discourage cartel and monopolistic business practices and business
arrangements which result in restricting production and increasing
prices or which curtail international trade, to encourage competition
and productivity, and to facilitate and stimulate the growth of international trade by reducing barriers which may hamper such trade
when the attainment of the agreed program may be affected . . . ."

Spain also committed itself to assist the United States in "observing and reporting on labor conditions in Spain as these relate to the aims and operations of the Mutual Security program. . . ." This was a strong commitment for Spain, but it would hardly have satisfied the International Labor Organization, let alone the AFL/CIO in the United States.

In one respect, at least, the United States drove a hard bargain with Spain. Under the formula of the Marshall Plan, the United States' dollars advanced for economic assistance required payments of equivalent amounts of local currency by aid-receiving governments into specially designated and blocked central bank accounts. Of these "counterpart funds," releasable only by joint agreement, ninety percent was usually to be used for the economic development of the host country, and ten percent was reserved for U.S. administrative expenses in that country. However, in Spain the United States retained sixty percent of the counterpart funds for local expenses of the Base Construction Program in addition to reserving the normal ten percent for its own administrative expenses. This left only thirty percent for economic projects in Spain. This formula lasted until 1958, at which time Spain began to receive ninety percent of the counterpart funds.

The Spanish government also agreed to accept a Special Economic Mission and to accord its personnel the privileges and immunities accorded to embassy personnel of comparable rank. Under the parlance of the Mutual Security Act of 1951, the mission was to be called the "United States Operation Mission," headed by a director. The structure and organization of this mission differed somewhat in Spain from missions with comparable roles elsewhere, and it will be described in some detail in a subsequent passage.

Article 3 of the Economic Aid Agreement covered investment guarantees. However, such guarantees were not automatic, each case requiring the approval of the government of Spain as well as that of the United States. The guarantees were intended to cover potential loss due to expropriation, revolution, or some similar extraordinary circumstance where the American investor lost his capital investment through no fault of his own. As it turned out, this article was nothing more than a "hunting license." To obtain from Spain the individual investment guarantee for the American investors turned out to be tedious work.

The third agreement, the Mutual Defense Assistance Agreement, covered the details for providing military assistance by the United States to Spain. Four of the seven articles imposed mutual obligations on both governments: to make available to each other, and to such other governments as they might agree upon, such materials and services as might be agreed upon; to exchange patent rights, to promote peace, and to abide by the agreement until its termination on one year's notice. The responsibility was vested in Spain for the execution of the other three articles: to make peseta currency available to the United States; to admit U.S. personnel as part of the American embassy; and to cooperate with the United States in controlling trade with nations that threatened world peace.

The admission of U.S. personnel as part of the American embassy, as was done in other European countries which received assistance under the Marshall Plan, was significant. The United States maintained two principal military groups attached to the embassy. One was called JUSMG (Joint U.S. Military Group), which was responsible for coordinating the entire military construction program in Spain. It, in turn, was under the command of USCINCEUR (U.S. Commander-in-Chief, Europe), who was the executive agent of the Department of Defense for administering the base program in Spain. The other military group attached to the embassy was known as JUSMAAG (Joint U.S. Military Assistance Advisory Group). It performed advisory functions similar to the MAAGS in countries throughout the world that received U.S. military assistance.

A third military group, not under the American Embassy in Spain, was that responsible for military operations. For the Air Force, that control was in the Headquarters of the 16th Air Force, and for the Navy, in the Naval Operations Office in Washington.

It should be stressed that the overall diplomatic responsibility for the conduct of U.S. policy in Spain was vested in the American ambassador in Madrid. He was the chairman, in effect, of the country team, consisting of himself, the director of the U.S. Operations Mission, and the single person, a high-ranking Air Force officer, usually a major general, who headed both JUSMG and JUSMAAG.

LOCATION OF BASES

For some inexplicable reason, the bases were located close to several of Spain's major cities. The principal air base, Torrejón, was placed only sixteen miles from the national capital, Madrid. The second most important air base, called Sanjuruo-Valenzuela, was placed six miles from Zaragoza, which is northeast of Madrid and Spain's fifth largest city. The deepwater naval base at Rota, designed to handle the Navy's largest vessels, particularly submarines, was placed only six miles from one of Spain's most important seaports, Cadiz. The third important air base, Morón, is only 37 miles from Sevilla, Spain's fourth largest city. Whitaker states that Franco himself reportedly chose the Torrejón location, partly for convenience when the Americans would depart Spain, and partly for the propaganda effect to show that Spain had joined the United States in defense of the West.[3]

At first there was no complaint, at least in public, regarding the vulnerability of Spain's cities by virtue of the location of the bases. However, in the wake of the 1957 launching of Sputnik by the Soviets, important discussions were held between representatives of the two governments as to whether some relocation plan might be considered. By that time, of course, the bases were almost completed. What is known is that a high level mission from the United States engaged in a discussion with the Spaniards in early 1958. On April 28, 1958, Franco wrote a letter to Secretary Dulles stressing the importance of trying to accommodate public opinion regarding the inherent risks in the base locations. Franco also brought up in the letter, almost as an afterthought, the subject of U.S. economic aid, "until now inadequate," to use his own words. By then it was too late, and the bases became operational in 1959. The four main bases ultimately cost about $420 million, with counterpart pesetas contributing about one-third of the cost, and the balance being paid directly by the United States. Here it should be remembered that the counterpart funds actually were generated by American dollars contributed to the Economic Aid Program.[4]

The pace of construction of the bases was deliberate. This was caused by a combination of at least five factors. First, Spain was the latest in a worldwide chain of bases available to the United States. The national security factor was urgent as always, but it did not require a "crash basis" construction.

Second, the Department of Defense, working through the Department of the Navy and the latter's Bureau of Yards and Docks, had learned to economize through a complicated process of subcontracting. It engaged three major firms as prime contractors: Brown and Root of Houston, Raymond International of New York City, and the Walsh Construction Company of Davenport, Iowa, resulting in a firm known as Brown-Raymond-Walsh. This firm, in turn, engaged several subcontractors to perform various parts of the actual construction.

Third, the contractors were ordered to use construction equipment salvaged from the base construction program in Morocco, 1951-1952. This equipment was in good condition, generally speaking, but there was considerable delay in carrying out the salvage process.

Fourth, it was determined to use Spanish labor in the construction program. A major, time-consuming effort was required to train these workers, even though, once trained, the capability of the Spanish worker was high. Spain provided 5000 workers directly employed in the base program, and another 15,000 indirectly through Spanish subcontractors, according to Benjamin Welles.[5] Beside the jobs and income derived from the construction program, Spanish industry acquired important technology and know-how in the use of modern, sophisticated equipment and gained ownership of an estimated $30 million worth of such equipment when the construction program was completed.

Besides the four major bases described above, Spain also was the site of several smaller ones, which were, of course, later to be taken over by the Spanish themselves. An Air Force fighter base was built at Reus (southwest of Barcelona) and a supply and communications base was constructed near Sevilla, at San Pablo. The Air Force also maintained seven radar aircraft and warning sites, one on the island of Mallorca, just off the east coast of Spain, and six on the mainland. Once the Spaniards had acquired the know-how to operate these bases, they were manned entirely by Spanish Air Force personnel. The northern port of El Ferról, in northwestern Spain, was the site of a U.S. Navy Oil Storage and Supply Center. This also happened to be the native city of Franco. The Navy also built an ammunition storage depot at Cartagena, on the Mediterranean coast. These facilities were to become important supply bases for the Spanish Navy later.[6]

Linking all of the bases to the port at Cadiz was the strategically vital petroleum pipeline, extending 485 miles from the Rota Naval Base to the Zaragoza Air Base northwest of Madrid. Without the pipeline, the bases would have never become functional. According to Whitaker, a source in the Strategic Air Command stated in 1958 that "a Wing of B-47's consumes in an afternoon more fuel than the entire Spanish Tanker Fleet can transport in a month."[7]

By the time the bases were operational in 1959, the U.S. military personnel in Spain had reached a total of 7,000 to 8,000. With their family members, the total number of American military personnel approximated 15,000. Rubottom, who lived in Spain from 1953 to 1956, recalls that there was excellent rapport between Spaniards and Americans. At first, most Americans lived in Spanish housing, but gradually they were assimilated into the base housing as the units were completed. The thorny religious problem proved less serious than expected, according to Welles.[8] The senior American chaplain at each base was a Roman Catholic, responsible for liaison with local Spanish Catholic authorities.

U.S.-SPANISH ECONOMIC COOPERATION

In word and deed, the Economic Agreement signed on September 26, 1953, was one that called for "cooperation." American personnel involved in the program learned to avoid the words "aid" and "assistance" which were common in the U.S. economic mission terminology. They learned that Spanish officials were sensitive to the concept of U.S. contributions as assistance. And before long they realized that the program was indeed a two-way street that required "cooperation." Officials in both governments knew that the base agreements and the defense support agreement stemmed from a mutual need, and that their governments had struck a deal.

By the economic agreement the United States was authorized to establish a Special Economic Mission. Under the leadership of Ambassador Dunn, and with the support of the Foreign Operations Administration (its successor today is known as the Agency for International Development), and the Department of State, the United States Operations Mission (USOM) in Spain had two distinctive features:

1. it was small, with only 23 officers and additional supporting staff; and
2. it was a "combined economic mission," integrating the staffs of the special mission and the economic section of the American Embassy of Madrid.

The decision to keep the mission small was based on hard lessons learned in Greece, in Korea, and in the administration of the Marshall Plan. While the Defense Support Program for Spain was not as large as some of those, it was, nonetheless, fifth in size of the programs in Europe. Both Ambassador Dunn and the mission directors had to resist suggestions from Washington to enlarge the personnel of USOM.

The fact that the Spaniards, too, kept their numbers small, made it easier for the Americans to hold the line. As for the "combined economic mission," this pattern had been tried in other countries with but little success. Ambassador Dunn, with years of experience in Rome and in Paris, where the American economic missions had grown to swollen proportions, was determined to use his economic personnel efficiently. This view was shared by Edward Williams, a New York insurance executive who took over the directorship of USOM shortly after the agreements were signed, replacing George Train. This efficient personnel plan was adhered to by subsequent directors of USOM in Spain, and became a model for economic missions opened up in other countries in subsequent years.[9]

The mission was divided into the following sections:

1. economic analysis and planning;
2. industrial sector, including electric power and steel;

3. minerals and mining;
4. agriculture;
5. technical assistance;
6. commercial sector;
7. transport, including highways, railways, and maritime.

The section heads developed contacts all over Spain, including government officials, the managers of government-owned corporations, and the managers of private industries. While the approval for a particular allocation of funds for, say, the purchase of railroad ties for RENFE (the government-owned railway system) had to be approved by the Spanish mission in Madrid, the detailed negotiations leading to the purchase were carried out with officials at RENFE.

There was no shortage of problems at the beginning of the program of economic cooperation. Patience was as much an asset as experience and expertise. Those Americans who did not speak Spanish with relative fluency either took lessons or, if they already knew French or Italian, quickly learned Spanish on the job. In such a setting, language facility was an indispensable tool. It speeded up the work, lessened the possibility of misunderstanding, and it conveyed an interest to one's counterpart that no other action could do. This was true even when the counterpart spoke English, as many Spaniards did.

While Spain did not have the latest equipment and technology in 1953, the country had done amazingly well with its limited resources. Spaniards had native ingenuity, but they were also eager to have the latest know-how and technology. During the height of the technical exchange program, more than a hundred Americans visited Spain, ranging from practitioners of the vocational skills to advanced scientists and university professors. One of the first visitors was an atomic scientist from Columbia University who lectured at the Physics Institute at the University of Madrid. He spoke fluent Spanish and attracted an enthusiastic audience for his lectures. Another visitor was a craftsman skilled in the making of shoes who visited plants in Spain. Leather goods, especially shoes, are a leading Spanish export. Visitors to Spain under the technical exchange program were not limited to Americans. One who left a major impact was an Austrian economist who spent several weeks in Spain to help the government design its first system of national economic accounts.

The Economic Cooperation Program required inspections and site visits. These were carried out jointly by American and Spanish personnel. Rubottom found Spaniards proud and friendly when he visited every region of the country to see at first hand steel mills, hydroelectric dams, railway improvements, soil conservation projects, and a wide range of industrial plants.

The mutual euphoria of 1953 soon gave way to the probing and testing that was inevitable between new partners like Spain and the United States. The kind of close cooperation that was required, and that eventually did prevail, was not automatic, nor did it come easily to either side. While the agreements spelled out plan and intent, they could not force understanding nor good will on the part of the human beings involved. Those individuals could not easily discard their backgrounds nor their prejudices. At times it was a love-hate relationship. To some Americans the Spaniards could do no wrong, and vice versa. In these cases, it was difficult to obtain any objective judgment. In contrast, there were others for whom no concession was enough. The "other" side could not be trusted, and any kind of agreement on a project was elusive until instructions came down from higher authority. It devolved on the ambassadors and the mission directors to find the balance.

The personal equation, that is, the mix of experience, personality, and position to be found in particular individuals was the key. The responsible American officials dealt primarily with the Spanish Minister of Commerce, Manuel Arburua, a friendly, urbane, and experienced international banker. However, certain kinds of projects required the participation and involvement of the Minister of Industry, Planell, the Minister of Agriculture, Cavestani, and the Director of the National Institute of Industry, Suances. Cavestani was notably cooperative and took a personal interest in the wide variety of projects that sharply and favorably impacted on Spain's long-neglected agricultural sector. Suances had been a classmate of General Franco in military school, and everybody knew it. The institute which he headed, with responsibility for the government-owned enterprises, had an insatiable appetite for funds. American officials were not opposed to assisting vital government projects, such as the INI steel complex at Áviles, but they were determined that the private sector should also get its fair share. Often they found themselves supporting Spain's bankers and heads of large private enterprises in the latter's quest for funds that would enable them to modernize and expand.

At the working level the Spanish government relied on those of its career diplomats who had commercial and economic experience in posts abroad. To match the "combined" operations or economic mission of the United States, the Spanish government created the Directorate-General of Economic Cooperation under the direction of the Under-Secretary of Foreign Economy who reported to both the Ministry of Foreign Affairs and the Minister of Commerce. The first Director-General was José Antonio Gimenez Arnau, who held the post until February 1956. He was succeeded by his assistant, Juan José Rovira, who remained in that position for several years before he became Spanish ambassador in Washington. In October 1957 the office was reorganized and Rovira's title became Director-General, Office of Agreements with North America. Gradually, as Spain became more self-sufficient, and as it developed its traditional trading relationships with other Western European countries following the Stabilization Agreement of 1959, the work of the USOM and its Spanish counterpart declined in importance. In 1964 the Spanish government eliminated its special office and divided the remainder of its responsibilities among various ministries.

The American ambassador set the example for the members of his team. As has been mentioned earlier, Ambassador James Dunn was peerless in his leadership of the mission during the first 18 months after the signing of the Pact of Madrid. His successor was Ambassador John Davis Lodge, who remained in Madrid until the Kennedy administration assumed office in 1961. Lodge's six-year tenure was unusual for an American chief of mission. He was outspoken in his support of the U.S.-Spanish connection, and when teamed with Senator McCarran in Washington, they made a politically influential combination. Of the two ambassadors, Dunn was the archetype career diplomat—intelligent, experienced, low-key, patient, thorough, and polished. Lodge was the archetype politically inclined ambassador—intelligent, experienced, intuitive, sensitive, impatient and aggressive. They both performed the compulsory routine well, entertaining Spanish government officials, fellow diplomats, and the titled families of Spain. In matters of style, however, Dunn and Lodge were completely different in temperament and in their choice of friends. Even in the persons of the ambassadors, therefore, Spaniards could see "many faces of America."

The American representation in Spain was not limited to the diplomatic and military missions. There was a small but elite corps of American business representatives there, many of whom remained in Spain during the difficult days of war and deprivation. Their Spanish contacts, and their experience, were to prove invaluable to the U.S. mission when the connection was turned on. Outstanding among this group was George Dennis, who went to Spain in the late 1920s to work for IT&T, and who, in retirement, still resides in Madrid with his wife, Amarie Dennis, a widely respected scholar and author.

THE ECONOMIC INPUTS

The Spanish government understood that the conclusion of the Pact of Madrid was simply the beginning of another phase of a continuing campaign to obtain the maximum possible American financial and military support. The controlled press and the public, to a modest degree, expressed pleasure that the agreements had been signed because they signaled (1) that the quarantine of Spain had been lifted, and (2) that assistance was on the way to alleviate the distressing economic situation. However, Spanish officials had no time for euphoria. Their challenge was two-fold: first, to establish a sound and cooperative relationship with the members of the American mission in Madrid, whose recommendations would greatly influence the amount and the terms of future allocations in Spain; and, second, to continue to influence key American leaders in Washington, primarily in the Congress where the purse strings of appropriations were held.

The agreements themselves did not promise specific amounts of aid, either military or economic, any more than they detailed the base facilities to be provided by Spain. Official announcements in both countries, nonetheless, mentioned a sum of $226 million as support to be provided Spain under the terms of the U.S. Mutual Security Act during the U.S. fiscal year 1953/54, and, of this, $85 million was to be for defense support (that is, economic) assistance and $141 million was to be for the purchase of military end-use items. [10] Angel Viñas, however, having researched classified materials on the subject in Madrid, has said that the pledge of 1953/54 was subsequently raised to $465 million in confidential letters exchanged between Foreign Minister Artajo and Ambassador Dunn in Madrid. [11] Of this total, $350 million was to be military support and $115 million economic support.

There was speculation at the time as to whether the United States had made a commitment to Spain for the second as well as the first agreement year, that is, for fiscal year 1954/55 as well as 1953/54. While in fact no specific commitment was made, many Spanish officials seemed to believe that in the second year they would receive as economic support no less than the $85 million grant formally announced for the first year of the pact. Furthermore, they expected to receive it again as a grant, not as a loan.

After delay, the executive branch of the American government acknowledged a $30 million commitment of economic support to Spain for 1954/55 but no more. When the congressional lobby in behalf of Spain cranked up its big guns, nevertheless, in connection with the 1954/55 appropriation bill, Spain was earmarked in the legislation for $85 million, of which $55 million would be a grant of Public Law 480 funds, and $30 million would be regular defense support. Thus, agencies of the executive branch, including the Department of State and the Foreign Operations Administration in Washington, and the mission in Madrid, were unfortunately made to appear unresponsive to Spain's needs, at best, or plain anti-Franco, at worst. Some in Spain said the country's friends appeared to be in the Congress.

But Spanish officials involved with administration of the program were rapidly growing in sophistication concerning processes of the American government. Both Spanish and American administrators shared continuing problems: (1) dividing up a "pie" that was always too small for the need, and (2) explaining to diplomats of other countries that were equally as important as Spain to U.S. security and political interests why Spain should be singled out by name for special consideration in U.S. appropriations.

Another sensitive question arose at that time. Whose responsibility in the United States government was it to conduct relations with the Spanish government, that of the executive branch or the Congress? The constitution states that the responsibility lies with the executive branch. In most cases that prerogative is unchallenged. The president makes the major policy decisions, then delegates the responsibility to the Secretary of State, who, in turn, directs the activities of his principal assistants and the operating arms of foreign policy. By the late 1950s, the practices in connection with European assistance programs had become ritualistic. The Assistant Secretary of State for European Affairs and the Regional Director for Europe of the Foreign Operations Administration testified before the respective congressional committees each fiscal year formally to request the global aid packages for Europe that had been carefully put together after weighing all the political-economic nuances. The testimony of these officials reflected the opinions of the missions in the field and those of the most experienced bureaucrats in Washington, and usually those recommendations were accepted with few changes.

The Spanish case, however, was always different. Again the principal actor was Senator McCarran who, after leading the campaign to restore normal relations with Spain, remained a determined advocate for the maximum amount of assistance for Spain. Until his death, McCarran was the voice of Spain in the Congress. Even more remarkable was his success, as the figures reveal, notwithstanding the lack of any U.S. commitment beyond three years.

CONGRESSIONAL TRAVEL TO SPAIN

Members of Congress did not vote blindly for the annual appropriations to assist Spain. They traveled to Spain to see the country at first hand, starting in 1949. While at first there was only a handful, the flow built up to a steady stream by the mid-1950s. Nearly all had good reason to come since they served on committees with wide-ranging responsibilities, such as Foreign Relations, Appropriations, Armed Services, Ways and Means, Agriculture, Commerce, and Labor.

The members had a legitimate interest, indeed curiosity, about Spain, and so did their constituents who, for almost two decades, had heard mainly a steady rhythm of criticism of Franco Spain, especially if they were a part of the Protestant majority of the United States. Senior staff members of the various congressional committees invariably accompanied the members, so that it was not unusual to have a group of ten to twenty to visit Spain. They came, they saw, and they were very often conquered by the Spaniards. This era of good feeling in the Congress toward Spain lasted until the mid-1960s.

The term "junket" has come to be used pejoratively in reference to congressional travel abroad. The characterization is in some, perhaps many, cases appropriate, but the typical congressional visit to Spain during 1953-1965 (Rubottom's tenure there) was a constructive one. Spain had not been prominent in U.S. foreign relations since the end of the nineteenth century, so the members needed to receive the detailed briefings they got in Madrid reflecting the sudden upgrading of Spain on the American priority list. They also saw and felt that nation's economic distress. Their supportive votes back in Washington, in retrospect, should not have been surprising.

Congressional visitors had one financial advantage. Their "tourist dollar" came out of counterpart funds, which required no accountability. These funds could be drawn legally from American embassies in all of the Marshall Plan countries, and once the Pact of Madrid was signed in September 1953, counterpart funds were available in Spain.

The discussions in the Congress regarding the amount of funds earmarked for Spain and the conditions attached to them were always featured in the Spanish press. Like virtually all countries which have received U.S. assistance, Spain could make the case that its allocations were insufficient for its needs. Spain's case was strengthened when its allocations were compared to the amounts received by other recipients like those in the Marshall Plan. Even though the Spanish economic mission was discreet, it argued its case for more assistance forcefully. Then, in 1954, shortly after the pact was signed, a Spanish-made film, Bienvenida, Mr. Marshall!,[12] was widely distributed in Spain. It depicted a vehicle carrying Marshall speeding through a Spanish village where the peasants had been waiting expectantly; the vehicle left nothing but dust and dashed hopes behind. Poignant though it was, the film aroused no hostility. Perhaps that was because it was not long before villages like the one in the film got some practical benefit out of the "connection." Spain had had relatively good highways since the 1920s, radiating out from Madrid to the four corners of the peninsula like the spokes of a wheel, but they had badly deteriorated during the civil war, the Second World

TABLE 2-1

U.S. ECONOMIC SUPPORT TO SPAIN DURING PERIOD OF INITIAL DEFENSE TREATY, FISCAL YEARS 1954-63
(millions of dollars)

	U.S. Fiscal Years										
	1953/ 1954	1954/ 1955	1955/ 1956	1956/ 1957	1957/ 1958	1958/ 1959	1959/ 1960	1960/ 1961	1961/ 1962	1962/ 1963	Total
Defense Support Assistance	85.0	60.0	70.0	56.1	51.1	46.0	36.0	15.0		—	504.2
U.S. agricultural surplus products	14.0	55.0	27.0	18.0	22.8	18.0	15.0	32.0	—	—	(201.8)
Technical assistance	0.4	0.6	2.0	1.0	1.1	1.1	1.0	1.0	1.5	—	(9.6)
Nonagricultural products	70.6	29.4	31.0	51.0	32.2	32.0	30.0	3.0	13.5	—	(292.7)
Public Law 480 (sales of farm surplus commodities)	20.0[a]	47.1	71.8	66.8[b]	111.6	96.4	64.0	49.5		—	572.2
Social Assistance (National Catholic Welfare Conference – Caritas)[c]	5.0	22.0	31.0	35.0	25.6	10.8	14.2	11.4	11.2	10.9	177.1
SUBTOTAL	110.0	154.1	162.8	171.8	193.3	158.3	124.2	96.9	26.2	10.9	
Development Loan Fund						17.2					17.2
Export-Import Bank[d,e]	48.1	10.9	3.3	9.8	4.3	8.0	41.2	49.7	41.7	31.6	297.0[e]
TOTAL ECONOMIC SUPPORT[e]	158.1	165.0	166.1	181.6	197.6	183.5	165.4	146.6	67.9	42.5	1,522.7[e]
Military End-item Assistance	141.0										538.0[f]

[a] Special wheat sale for nonconvertible pesetas, 1953/54.

[b] Of this figure, $7 million proceed from U.S. agricultural surpluses solid in triangular trade to Austria and Switzerland, from which countries Spain imported manufactured goods.

[c] Calendar years, 1954-1963.

[d] Data for 1953/54 through 1958/59 from Angel Viñas et al., Política Comercial Exterior en España, 1931-1975 (Madrid: Banco Exterior de España, 1979), Quadro 13, p. 745. Data for 1959/60 through 1963/63 from Banco Urquijo, The Spanish Economy, 1963 (Madrid, 1964), p. 31.

[e] Annual figures do not sum to decade total because of unexplained omission of $48.4 million of Export-Import Bank loans from annual figures. Decade total reported in Banco Urquijo, The Spanish Economy, 1963, p. 31, is the same as that reported in Angel Viñas, "American Assistance to Spain: The Pact of Madrid, 1953-1963" (mimeographed, undated), p. 12.

[f] Total on June 30, 1962. Angel Viñas, "American Assistance to Spain" (mimeographed, undated), p. 17.

Source: Unless otherwise indicated, data are from Banco Urquijo, Servicio de Estudios, The Spanish Economy, 1954-1956 (Madrid, 1957); The Spanish Economy, 1961 (Madrid, 1962); and The Spanish Economy, 1963 (Madrid, 1964).

War, and the eight years of Spain's enforced isolation. Much of the highway maintenance work was performed by hand labor, in many cases by women who used long-handled sledge hammers to break boulders into rock and gravel needed for road foundations. By late 1954 modern machinery and equipment was being used to rebuild Spain's highways, freeing women workers to do other necessary but less onerous work.

SIGNIFICANCE OF U.S. SUPPORT

Eventually, the U.S. economic support provided Spain during the entire decade of the first defense and economic agreements came to about $1,690 million, and military assistance came to about $521 million. Various sources provide slightly different totals.

Year by year figures that were provided to Banco Urquijo by the U.S. embassy in Madrid as the program progressed, for example, shown in Table 2-1, give the economic support to be about $1,523 million. According to these figures, appropriations through the Mutual Security Agency and successor agencies, known as "defense support assistance," amounted to $504 million in the decade; sales of U.S. agricultural surplus commodities for pesetas under Public Law 480 totaled another $527 million; and economic aid provided by the U.S. government through the National Catholic Welfare Conference, in combination with the Spanish organization Caritas, came to $177.1 million. Although not properly characterized as official aid related to the joint agreements, the credits provided Spain by the U.S. Export-Import Bank and the Development Loan Fund constituted a further important source of external funding, and together amounted during the decade to $214 million.

Data from the Office of Business Economics, U.S. Department of Commerce, indicate a slightly higher total for economic support than those of the Banco Urquijo (the total is $1,688 million as compared to the Banco Urquijo's $1,523 million), and they show slightly less ($521 million as compared to $538 million) than Angel Viñas has reported for military support (see Table 2-1). The Office of Business Economics figures are shown in Tables 2-2 and 2-3.

The commodity and service composition of the aid provided as defense support assistance and under Public Law 480 during the first few years of the treaty are indicated in Table 2-4. It will be seen that 30 percent of the combined aid consisted of cotton and another 10 percent was cottonseed oil. Machinery and vehicles of ferrous and nonferrous metals made up another 12 percent. Three percent was coal and other fuels. The dollar cost of technical

TABLE 2-2

NONMILITARY GRANTS, CREDITS, AND OTHER ASSISTANCE, UNITED STATES TO SPAIN,
BY U.S. FISCAL YEARS, 1951/55–1963 (millions of dollars)

	1951/55	1956	1957	1958	1959	1960	1961	1962	1963	Total
Net grants, credits, and other assistance	140	117	135	78	118	58	115	60	2	823
Net grants[a]	27	42	49	50	33	25	26	54	19	325
Gross grants	38	79	104	102	62	40	35	57	23	540
Less: reverse grants and returns	10	37	55	53	29	15	10	3	4	216
Net credits[a]	56	31	8	4	50	43	51	62	61	366
New credits	79	32	10	7	55	48	57	69	73	430
Less: principal collections	23	1	2	4	5	5	6	7	12	65
Net other assistance[a,b]	57[c]	44	78	25	35	-10	39	-56	-78	134
Foreign currency claims acquired	72[c]	95	130	82	125	58	94	54	8	718
Less: currency disbursed	15[c]	51	52	58	90	68	56	110	86	586
Gross assistance	189	206	244	191	242	146	186	180	104	1,688
Grants	38	79	104	102	62	40	35	57	23	540
Credits	79	32	10	7	55	48	57	69	73	430
Other assistance	72	95	130	82	125	58	94	54	8	718

[a] Totals may differ from sums of subclasses because of rounding.
[b] Chiefly undisbursed counterpart funds arising from sale for pesetas of agriculture commodities.
[c] 1954/55.

Source: U.S. Department of Commerce, Foreign Grants and Credits by the United States, Fiscal Year Reports 1957-1963.

46

TABLE 2-3

SUMMARY, U.S. FOREIGN ASSISTANCE TO SPAIN
JULY 1, 1945–JUNE 30, 1963
(millions of dollars or equivalent)

Military supplies and services			
Gross grants	521		
Less: reverse grants and returns	—		
Net total		521	
Other aid			
Grants			
Gross grants (adjusted)	542		
Less: reverse grants and returns	177		
Net grants (less conversions)		365	
Credits			
Gross credits	431		
Less: principal collections	65		
Net credits (including conversions)		365	
Other assistance (through net accumulation of foreign currency claims)			
Currency claims acquired	719		
Less: currency used	584		
Net other assistance		135	
Total net assistance		1,386	
Total gross assistance			2,213
Military supplies and services			521
Other aid (economic and technical assistance)			1,692

Source: U.S. Department of Commerce, Foreign Grants and Credits by the United States Government, Fiscal Year 1963, Table 2A, pp. 5-9.

assistance was about three-quarters of one percent of the total program in those early years.

Any effort to divide the U.S. assistance program into amounts that were "loans" and amounts that were "grants" is somewhat arbitrary since any loan which is provided at less than market terms is in part a grant, and any grant which gives rise to local counterpart funds which are then used for the interest of the grantor is a gift that has had to be partially repaid. To compare the two, one must discover

TABLE 2-4

COMPOSITION OF U. S. SUPPORT UNDER THE DEFENSE
SUPPORT PROGRAM AND PUBLIC LAW 480
IN EARLY PROGRAM YEARS

Commodity or Service Classification	Amounts Authorized under Defense Support Program up to March 31, 1957	Amounts Authorized under Public Law 480 up to March 31, 1956	Total
Food, feed, and fertilizer	32,837,681	36,209,000	69,046,681
Grains	2,345,995	4,809,000	
Other	30,491,686		
Cottonseed oil		30,000,000	
Potatoes		1,400,000	
Coal and other fuel	8,494,167		8,494,167
Raw materials and semifinished goods	123,602,256	10,951,900	134,554,156
Cotton	80,432,086	8,736,900	
Nonferrous metals and products	12,062,859		
Iron and steel mill materials and products	23,409,063		
Other	7,698,248		
Tobacco		2,215,000	
Machinery and vehicles	70,556,005		70,556,005
Machinery and equipment	60,869,472		
Vehicles and other transportation equipment	9,686,533		
Miscellaneous and unclassified	2,104,205		2,104,205
Rubber and rubber products	2,064,205		
Scientific apparatus	40,000		
Noncommodity group	11,868,292	2,503,908	14,372,200
Freights	10,618,292	2,503,908	
Other	1,250,000		
Technical Assistance	2,289,032		2,289,032
Total	251,751,645	49,664,808	301,416,446

Source: Banco Urquijo, Servicio de Estudios, The Spanish
Economy, 1954-56 (Madrid, 1957), pp. 88, 90.

the economic gain obtained by the receiver of the funds for the
period involved.[13] Unfortunately, data are not available for esti-
mating this in a careful way. Some hypothetical calculations, however, illustrate the principle.

According to data in Table 2-2, the economic aid provided Spain
in the calendar years 1951-1963 totaled $1,688 million. If we assume
that "other assistance" largely took the form of grants, grant-aid
constituted 74.5 percent of the assistance while loans comprised

25.5 percent. It is known that all of the grants, except those to Caritas, required the deposit of counterpart pesetas, some of which were then used for expenses of U.S. programs in Spain. The loans of the Export-Import Bank had maturities varying from five to fifteen years, were repayable in equal semiannual installments, and carried a rate of interest varying from 5.15 to 5.75 percent.

Some crude estimates suggest an order of magnitude of the value of these transfers to Spain. With regard to the loans, a large part of which were from the Export-Import Bank, assume that all were ten-year loans at 5.5 percent, that the flow to Spain was in equal increments over a ten-year period beginning in 1953, and that each loan was repaid on a ten-year straight-line time basis. Assume, too, that the marginal social value in Spain of the capital in that period was 7.5 percent so that Spain enjoyed a 2 percent social gain on the use of the capital. In that case, Spain had the use of borrowed sums over a nineteen-year period that were as high as $236 million in year ten and as low as $4.3 million in year 19 when the last loan was paid off. Such a flow of capital available to Spain would have yielded net earnings over the 19 years of $47.3 million, and the flow would have had a present value at the beginning of 1953 (discounted at the assumed social return of 7.5 percent) of $26.53 million. The loans represented, therefore, something like a lump sum gift of $26.53 million at the beginning of 1953.[14]

The flow of grants, if it had been made in equal increments over ten years, would have given Spain the use of a sum growing at $125.8 million a year. Assuming that 10 percent was returned to the grantor for administering the program, the flow (discounted at the assumed social return of 7.5 percent) would have had a value at the beginning of the decade of $777 million.

Taking the loans and grants together, then, such calculations put the value of U.S. economic assistance to Spain in the 1953-1962 decade in the area of that of a lump sum grant in 1953 of about $803 million. At an exchange rate of 39.577 pesetas per dollar,[15] this is 31,780 million pesetas or about 13.9 percent of Spain's 1953 national income.

This total, of course, includes the portion of the total that was diverted to construction of military bases, but it includes nothing for the value of military end-use aid provided as part of the program. Assuming that the military equipment and training had a value to Spain equal to its dollar cost, that $538 million of aid was transferred in equal installments during the decade, and that it, too, had a marginal social rate of return of 7.5 percent (in terms, say, of an improved sense of national security or through multiplier linkages to other production in Spain), that aid had a present value in 1953 of $369 million or 14,604 million pesetas. Adding this sum to the 1953 value of economic assistance, one finds that the total package had a possible 1953 value of 46,384 million pesetas, or about 20.3 percent of the 1953 Spanish national income. If the marginal social return on capital were indeed 7.5 percent, and if that rate were sustained for the thirty years following 1953 (the compound rate of overall growth in Spanish nominal GNP, 1954-1979, was 15.8 percent), the value of the U.S. 1953-1962 aid may have been, by 1983, $10,261 million or more than 1.2 trillion pesetas (at 121.239 per dollar).

There are, of course, many other ways to try to get some perspective on the significance of the U.S. support to Spain in conjunction with the 1953 agreements. The dollar value of the decade-long economic support (even taking it to be only 1,523 million), for example, was more than twice the value of Spain's total merchandise exports in any of the last four years of the period. Or, converted to pesetas at 1960's exchange rate, it was three-quarters of Spain's gross fixed capital formation in, say, 1960. Or, focusing on the size of the annual flows of aid, at a value of six to eight billion pesetas per year, they amounted to approximately a third of Spain's annual export earnings in each of the early years of the program, and, as shares of Spain's total annual government budgets, they were approximately one-eighth to one-fifth in the early years and one-ninth to one-eighth in the later years.

Of course, the assistance was tied to the purchase of U.S. commodities—to a great extent to the purchase of U.S. agricultural surplus commodities—and this meant that the value of the aid to Spain was less than if the same dollar values could have been used in any way that the aid recipient desired. It is not clear, however, what discount factor should be applied because of the use restrictions. Probably, it is not negligible. Frustrations were expressed from time to time in Spain concerning the military equipment, which was said to be insufficiently sophisticated and concerning the economic aid, which was said to consist too much of agricultural commodities rather than industrial machinery and equipment.

In general, the grant-aid—commodities, services, and technical information, and including freight costs—required the deposit of counterpart pesetas by the government of Spain in a special account created for that purpose at the Bank of Spain. The 1953 agreements specified that 10 percent of each deposit was to be placed at the disposal of the government of the United States for administration, and another 60 percent was to be available to the United States for the construction and maintenance of military bases in Spain; 30 percent was reserved for Spanish use. After 1958, 90 percent of annual contributions to counterpart funds were assigned to Spain. The agreement specified that, if Spain joined the International Monetary Fund (IMF) with a unified exchange rate, that exchange rate would be used

TABLE 2-5

SUMMARY OF COUNTERPART FUND ACCOUNT, 1954-1963
(millions of pesetas)

Calendar Years	In-Payments	Disbursements	Balance
1954	1,546	285	1,261
1955	3,500	650	4,111
1956	4,954	2,735	6,330
1957	6,011	3,603	8,738
1958	7,368	4,186	11,920
1959	5,501	6,587	10,834
1960	6,187	4,696	12,325
1961	6,740	8,648	10,416
1962	956	4,731	6,634
1963	1,731		
Total	44,494		

Source: Banco Urquijo, Servicio de Estudios, La Economia Española, volume for 1954-55 and annual volumes for 1956 through 1963.

to determine counterpart deposit obligations. Otherwise, the rate would be subject to negotiation. In the years prior to Spain's admission to IMF membership in 1959, several exchange rates were used.

Banco Hispano Americano and Banco Urquijo have recorded estimates through time of the buildup and disbursement of the counterpart funds. A summary is given in Table 2-5. Clearly, the in-payments to the account exceeded total disbursements from it during the first five years of the program, implying that the aid programs were holding down Spanish inflation in those years by increasing the availability of goods while draining off Spanish incomes and the Spanish money supply. In most subsequent years, the effects of the program were inflationary. As the counterpart balances were disbursed, they created a demand for domestic output that was financed with central bank money.

Use of a counterpart fund account in such a program of assistance results in the postponement of the determination of the final beneficiaries of the program. While the initial international grants result in the shipment of goods which are the once-for-all input to the recipient economy, since the users of those goods pay for them in local currency, those initial users are not the beneficiaries of the program. Their payments serve to finance those who subsequently receive goods or services at less than social cost thanks to payments charged to the counterpart account. Imports under the grants determine the benefits to the recipient nation; the allocation of counterpart funds determines the distribution within the nation.

Between a fourth and a third of the Spanish counterpart funds were directed to the construction and maintenance of the military bases provided for in the 1953 defense agreement. Hence, a part of what Spain got from the defense support allowances was the bases themselves. From the beginning, however, the Spanish government had the use of 30 percent of the counterpart funds, and after 1958, the share was raised to 90 percent. Hence, the use of approximately two-thirds of the total of the funds was ultimately at the disposal of the Spanish government. They were used to accelerate Spanish economic development in projects jointly approved by the two governments.

A study of the regional impact of the assistance programs would be interesting although it is largely beyond the scope of this survey. Certainly, the salutary effects were dispersed rather widely across Spain. Construction and operation of the air and sea bases at Rota (on the Bay of Cadiz, Cadiz Province), and the air bases at Zaragoza (Zaragoza Province), Torrejón (Madrid Province), and Morón de la Frontera (Sevilla Province), undoubtedly accelerated the growth of per capita income in those regions relative to the national norm, as did the major depots at Sevilla, El Ferról de Caudillo (La Coruña Province) and Cartagena (Murcia Province). Per capita income in all of the provinces involved, except Madrid and Zaragoza, was and still is well below the national average.[16] All of the provinces affected became strong centers of population growth in subsequent years,[17] and in all but Sevilla, income growth exceeded the national average between 1964 and 1977,[18] while Sevilla held its own. Regional development policies in the national development plans of the 1960s singled out La Coruña, Sevilla, and Zaragoza as "development poles" and were probably responsible for some of the advances there. The massive expenditures on the military bases, however, must also have made a contribution. The provision of raw foodstuffs and fibers under the economic support program improved welfare widely across Spain, and the programs of technical assistance surely accelerated the modernization of Spain's transport facilities and the nation's agricultural and industrial production.

Technical assistance, which rose from $400,000 a year in 1953, to $2 million in 1955/56, and then held at one million dollars or more in each of the fiscal years 1956/57 to 1961/62, took many forms, but was somewhat weighted toward the industrial sector. Approximately 50 percent of Spanish students and trainees who went to the United States and a like percentage of U.S. experts who visited

Spain were from the industry and mining sector. Of the trainees studying abroad, 18, 15, and 9 percent, respectively, came from agriculture, transport, and public administration. Altogether, 2,222 Spanish nationals studied or received training abroad, mostly in the United States, while 148 U.S. experts visited Spain. Twenty percent of the Spanish residents going abroad did work of an academic nature; the remaining 80 percent received training of an observational sort, some 60 percent spending less than two months abroad.[19]

Numerous Spanish government services received support in this program and several lasting services were created, including the National Industrial Productivity Service and the Industrial Management School. The Alcalá Center (for public administration) received support, as did the governmental agricultural advisory services.

While the United States was by no means the only contributor of technical assistance to Spain in this period, its contributions were the largest of any country. Programs administered by the OEEC/OECD (Organization for European Economic Cooperation/Organization for Economic Cooperation and Development) totaled nearly $1 million between 1960 and 1966, and bilateral programs other than that of the United States (especially Germany and France) came to perhaps $7 million.[20] The U.S. program totaled $9.6 million through the fiscal year 1961/62.

The economic support program, of course, affected the volume and direction of Spain's foreign commerce. The value and sources of imports were especially affected. Estimates in terms of U.S. dollars show total expenditures on imports of goods and services growing 54 percent, from $592.4 million in 1953 to $910.4 million in 1958, reflecting the transfer of U.S. financed goods. Exports, meanwhile, increased only 21 percent, from $574.5 to $694.4 million.[21] The share of merchandise imports originating in the United States grew from 12.0 to 26.2 percent between 1953 and 1956, and the share of Spanish exports taken by the United States grew from 6.9 to 13.3 percent. These changes, representing the special relationship between Spain and the United States in the late 1950s, have subsequently been largely reversed. As an import source, even in 1981, nevertheless, the United States remained by far Spain's largest single country supplier as a result of increased diversification of the sources of other Spanish imports.

Equally important to the trade changes in the 1950s and 1960s were the changes in foreign investment in Spain, about which more will be said later. Enormously significant, however, was the increase of U.S. investment after 1959, which amounted to an annual flow of 2.5 billion pesetas ($45 million) in 1965 (counting only those private investment projects in which the foreign participation exceeded 50 percent). U.S. investments constituted nearly half of all foreign investments made in Spain in that year,[22] and about 1.0 percent of Spain's gross capital formation.

IRONIES IN THE PACT

The Pact of Madrid was replete with ironies. One is that by the time of the signing in September 1953, an agreement was no longer as vital to the U.S. interest as it had appeared to be when Admiral Sherman visited Franco more than two years earlier. The Spaniards always tended to overvalue the pact in economic terms, and today's revisionists who criticize the pact as having compensated their country inadequately commit the same error. One might even suggest that, by prolonging the negotiations until late in 1953, the Spanish obtained agreements that were not as favorable to Spain as those that might have been had in 1952. From the U.S. standpoint, the Spanish bases were an extra dimension of Free World defense capability, useful and valuable up to a point, but never invaluable. As will be explained in some detail later, American strategic policy was subject to continuous review, and the review included the role and the worth of the Spanish bases.

It was also ironic that the U.S.-Spanish connection was just that, and nothing more. While the connection made Spain no longer a pariah among Western European and North American countries, it did not insure immediate reentry into the "family." Reentry had to be a slow and arduous climb, with the principal obstacle always Generalissimo Franco, who, until his death, remained an anathema to the northern European democracies.

Weeks throws light on two other ironies that emerged from the new relationship.[23] The military assistance program for Spain was justified as essential to enable Spanish armed forces to defend Spain from attack, "yet any reasonable analysis of international political realities leads to the conclusion that the only reason Spain was in any danger of attack was the fact that it harbored U.S. bases on its soil." In another vein he emphasizes a matter that, in his view, "is less easily proven but [that was] of potentially greater long-term importance for Spain." This is that the presence of American military equipment and training programs, functioning in association with the Spanish officers corps, "exposed them (particularly the [Spanish] Air Force and Navy) to the Western democratic norms of a professional military force which does not directly interfere in the nation's politics." Writing in 1977, and while pointing to no conclusive evidence of the result of the American example, Weeks thinks it clear that a relationship intended to be purely military might have influenced the attitude of Spanish officers "with profound political implications."

THE MANY FACES OF AMERICA

With the formalization of the "connection," starting in late 1953, Spanish officials learned what representatives of other nations with close American ties have learned—that their new partner was complex and multifaceted. Although protocol demanded that formal relations be conducted through official channels within the two governments, the Spaniards found themselves involved in a systemic process. To be sure, the American government was always present, and for Spain this meant both the executive branch and the legislative branch since the Spanish trump cards were still Senator McCarran and other influential members of Congress. The executive branch spoke with a profusion of voices. The Department of State, the Foreign Operations Agency, the Departments of Agriculture and Commerce, and the Export-Import Bank all had to be heard, and they were joined by the uniformed Pentagon branches—Army, Navy, and Air Force. Indeed, Spaniards learned that a reasonable list of U.S. agencies that required attention included the U.S. Information Agency, the Federal Aviation Administration, the Atomic Energy Commission, and others, which, at any given time, could become prominent actors in dealing with the Spanish government.

In the late 1940s and early 1950s, the sensitive voices of U.S. public opinion on Spain had consisted principally of the New York Times and the American religious community, especially the prominent voices of Protestantism. Their strong protests against closer ties with the Franco government had been neutralized by the congressional lobby and the growing cold war mentality of the American public. However, with the U.S.-Spanish connection turned on, a broader American public began to subject Spain, in all of its aspects, to close and, at times, harsher scrutiny.

Almost at once the press was not limited to New York, or New York and Washington. Rather the American democratic process was played out in Chicago, Des Moines, Houston, San Francisco, Boston, and Atlanta. Spain had to learn how to adjust to the media microscope focused on all parts of Spain, as in 1966 when four atomic bombs were inadvertently dropped near Palomares by an American plane. The adjustment was not easy because Spain itself had a rigidly controlled media under Franco, and some Spaniards were misled into thinking that the honeymoon period would last forever,

The business-financial-industrial community in the United States had, perhaps especially, to be considered. The intense competition between various entities could become embarrassing, but that also had its positive side. Through the competitive bidding process Spain got the most for its money. Both Spanish and American officials were sensitive to the importance of establishing sound precedents for contract-letting at the very outset of the program. By keeping the economic missions small, and placing responsibility and accountability in the hands of the respective directors, sound management practice was facilitated in the economic cooperation program. The base construction program, too, was kept manageable, partly as a result of limiting the general contracts to the joint-venture group of three firms with extensive overseas experience with large projects, namely the Brown-Raymond-Walsh group.

The AFL/CIO, as spokesman for organized labor in the United States, took an inordinate interest in Spain. It is difficult to identify the "party line" of labor, because, like so many groups in the United States, labor's viewpoint on Spain was ambivalent. George Meany, then at the zenith of his power as head of the AFL/CIO, was staunchly anticommunist and appreciated Spain's stand on the cold war. Yet he deplored the restrictions placed on Spanish labor, as did his cohorts, some of whom were publicly critical of the Franco regime.

One other American public sector group that became keenly interested in Spain was the academic community. Their curiosity ranged across the whole spectrum of disciplines because they had had little access to Spain during the decade of the Civil and Second World Wars. Most American scholars were profoundly anti-Franco and might have stayed away by choice. But with the passing of time, and the opening of the "connection" between the United States and Spain, they seemed to be willing to give the country another look. Many American professors happily participated in the cultural exchange programs. One of the most respected scholars of that era was Arthur P. Whitaker, Professor of Government at the University of Pennsylvania, whose book Spain and Defense of the West, published in 1961 by the Council on Foreign Relations and Harper's, remains an excellent source of information on the early years of post-World War II Spain. Whitaker first knew Spain in 1924 and observed it closely for nearly four decades under three governmental regimes. He treated Spain in his writing with the care and honesty of the artist, hiding nothing and struggling to avoid distortion.

"Think-tanks" began to assume prominence in the American academic community about the time the Pact of Madrid was signed. The results of their critiques and analyses were soon to be felt in Spain. The ink was hardly dry on the Pact of Madrid, for example, before the Rand Corporation published a study known as R-266, written by Albert Wohlstetter and other Rand associates, setting forth a method for the Air Force to select and utilize strategic bomber bases up to the year 1961.[24] Where did Spain fit in their analysis? The report stressed the coming vulnerability to Soviet first-strike capability of the then-planned system of American bombers based on advanced overseas bases, and recommended a second-strike retaliatory capability. The Spanish bases were meant to be intermediate overseas operating bases for B-47s, and the report labeled these bases as the worst of the four alternative basing systems considered, from the standpoint of both cost and vulnerability.

That report, obviously, did not crimp the "connection," which was only just beginning. It did, however, weaken the Spanish negotiating position for future allocations of U.S. funds in support of the agreements. It, also, in retrospect, evidences the cost, in terms of its negotiating position, to Spain of the long delay in completing the agreements.

Other views overlapped those of R-266 without accepting all of the conclusions. One of the most thought-provoking articles written during that time was by Townsend Hoopes, whose experience merited respect.[25] He served as assistant to the Secretary of Defense, 1948-1955, was consultant to the White House on overseas bases during the Eisenhower administration, and was to return as a senior Pentagon official in the Kennedy administration. While acknowledging that the Spanish bases, along with those in Canada, Guam, Japan, Okinawa, Newfoundland, England, and Morocco had been built to utilize the mid-range B-47 bomber, and were still strategically vital to U.S. defense, he added that "our strategic striking forces are moving gradually toward an independence of overseas bases, hastened by the developing Soviet ability to make them unusable for this purpose." Then, in a prophetic statement, given the role he later was to play in the Pentagon, Hoopes wrote, "The United States cannot avoid an early re-assessment of the overseas base system, of its assets and liabilities, and indeed of the fundamental substance and emphasis of the present strategic concept."

But Hoopes also held out a friendly and understanding hand to Spain, and indeed to all other nations with which the United States had, or would have, mutual defense arrangements. He pointed out "the need to grant meaningful compensation for our base rights," and urged the United States to utilize all forms of cooperation with other nations—military, economic, commercial, and technical—"on a continuing basis with intelligence and discrimination." Certainly this aspect of the Hoopes position is as valid for 1983 as it was for 1958. Acting on his principle, the United States can still hope to evoke support from its partners who are equally committed with it to the concept of freedom but whose effort in many cases requires sacrifice. The challenge in Spain for the United States after the Pact of Madrid was signed in 1953, was, as it remains, to enlarge the shared sense of mutual interest and mutual trust.

Rapid changes in strategic doctrine affecting the use of aircraft did not diminish the value of the Spanish bases for the short and medium term. The medium-range B-47 bomber was not phased out until 1965, and even then its replacement, the "shortlegged" B-58, which remained in Spain until 1968, required the base at Torrejón. When the long-range B-52 became operational, the Air Force counted on Spain to provide bases for their post-attack fueling, servicing, and landing— the only other full-service sites being the bases in England.

While analysts might question the value of the Spanish air bases, and Rand-266 did, nobody challenged the worth of the huge naval base at Rota. By the time it was completed in the late 1950s, the United States had a pressing need for a logistics, servicing, and repair base in the Mediterranean area for its missile-carrying submarines. According to Stephen S. Kaplan[26] the United States saved $24 million per year per submarine by basing those ships needed to protect NATO's southern flank at Rota so that they did not have to return (a 14-day round trip) every 56 days to Charleston or New London for replenishment and supply.

The naval air station runway at Rota also became valuable to the Air Force when the United States lost its SAC bases in Morocco in 1963. That runway was lengthened to SAC's specifications so that it could handle landings of B-52 bombers and KC-135 tankers in emergency situations.

Rota might have become a center of controversy over a sensitive issue—the presence of American nuclear weapons in Spanish territory—except for the common sense of the Spanish High Command which, apparently from the beginning, realized that such a presence would be one of the political costs of its connection with the United States. Polaris submarines began to use the Rota base in the early 1960s with Spain's acquiescence if not approval. The Air Force had no such luck. Following the 1966 incident over Palomares, it eventually agreed to fly no nuclear weapons over Spanish territory.

If the United States ever thought it might use the Spanish bases during the recurrent crises in the Middle East involving Israel, it was doomed to disappointment. In the June 1967 war, Washington was informed by the Spanish government that the bases could not be used for any American military involvement, although Americans evacuated from the Middle East were allowed to proceed through Spain. During the 1970 crisis in Jordan, Madrid again refused to permit the bases to be used for either employment or deployment of American armed forces.[27] Thus, Spain expressed its concern over its southern flank and its oil supply, and underscored its traditional friendship with the Arab bloc of nations.

THE "CONNECTION" AS LEVERAGE

Once the agreements were signed with the United States, Spain began gradually to emerge from its cocoon of isolation. It was like being admitted to a club in which, once the most powerful member had decided to vote affirmatively, the others refrained from using their blackball. Still it was a slow process. Spain joined the World Health Organization in 1951, UNESCO in 1952, and the International Labor Organization in 1953. Then began the carefully plotted campaign, with the United States as its principal ally, that brought it into the parent United Nations in 1955. While it was a deal with the Soviet Union that ultimately opened the U.N. door, Spain did its own part in cultivating the Arab and Latin-American blocs to supports its candidacy.

Spanish diplomacy could now concentrate on Western and Northern Europe, the area which was historically the best market for Spanish exports and the eastern boundary of NATO. Membership in NATO was to prove an elusive goal for Spain, and while the U.S. government (both the legislative and executive branches) would have been pleased to see Spain join, the United States in the end chose not to pressure its allies to accept Spain. Following 1953, after all, the latter was indirectly linked to NATO through the Pact of Madrid. [28] What was remarkable was that the United States finally had a truly national policy supportive of Franco Spain.

SPAIN AND THE OUTSIDE WORLD

Gibraltar

Spain could exist without Gibraltar but it does not choose to do so. Even if denied the physical possession of "the Rock," Spain keeps the issue of Gibraltar alive. As Welles describes it, Gibraltar is a "banderilla; it goads the Spanish pride." Gibraltar is also an issue of convenience that can be turned off and on.

During the 1950s and the 1960s the Gibraltar question tended to blow hot and cold, depending on whether Britain was being governed by the Laborites or the Conservatives. The Labor Party leaders, whether the older generation like Atlee and Bevan, or the younger generation, like Harold Wilson, simply had no stomach for Franco, so even the slightest hint of renewed Spanish interest in the Rock triggered an immediate and firm response. The Conservative leadership, which might have been expected to show more muscle, tended simply to "consider the source" and conduct business as usual without, of course, making any concession to the Spanish claims.

If nothing else, the Spaniards were persevering and tireless in bringing up the subject of Gibraltar. Foreign Minister Castiella in 1941 had first come to Franco's attention by co-authoring the book Revindicaciones de España along the Jose Maria Areilza. No claim was as important to him as that of Gibraltar. He made repeated visits to London to discuss the Gibraltar issue with his British counterpart. Whether it was the principal subject on his agenda or not, Castiella managed to bring up Gibraltar with the British government in 1959, 1960, and 1961. Finally, in 1963, Spain got the issue before the United Nations by charging the British with colonialism. From a public relations standpoint, Spain benefited from the U.N. discussion, but that had no influence on the British, who, then as now, refused to budge. The Spanish position is based on (1) Spain is a victim of British colonialism; (2) the local population of Gibraltar is of heterogeneous background without local roots; and (3) Gibraltar's income is derived entirely from the military base on the Rock and contraband trade at Spain's expense.[29]

The British appear to have played a cunning game with Gibraltar, opening up the subject if the Spaniards pressed hard and if it were on the agenda of the United Nations, but then closing the door when the pressure subsided. As in the case of the Falkland Islands, or Malvinas as they are called by the Argentines, it is the inhabitants of Gibraltar on whom the British rely to support their possession of the base. Even when Spain maneuvered a favorable vote at the U.N., it was always conditioned on the opinion expressed by the Gibraltarians who, in 1967, voted overwhelmingly to remain British (12,153 to 44 votes).[30]

Occasionally hopes have been raised for some kind of joint presence, if no co-sovereignty, of Britain and Spain in Gibraltar. However, Spanish initiatives over the years have been more irritating to the British than conducive to a gradual and long-term settlement of the Gibraltar question, the most glaring example being the Spanish action in closing the frontier at Algeciras in 1968, which in all likelihood proved more costly to the Spaniards than to the British. In light of the 1982 British-Argentine War of the Falklands (Malvinas), where Britain successfully fought to defend historical claims similar to those in Gibraltar, there seems little reason to expect soon a solution regarding the area favorable to Spain. However, Spain's admission to NATO in the summer of 1982 is one new and possibly encouraging factor in the Anglo-Spanish relationship.

Morocco

For centuries Spain maintained a substantial footing in northern and western Africa, the principal anchor having been Spanish Morocco.

However, by the time the U.S.-Spanish connection was turned on
in 1953, Spain's role as a colonial power had become counterproductive. To be placed in that category weakened the country's
case against Britain over Gibraltar and made it more difficult for
Spain to be admitted to the United Nations. Meanwhile, Morocco
itself was in a state of turmoil, subject to the rivalry of France and
Spain, both of which maintained large military garrisons there.
Franco, who had some expertise on North Africa from whence he
had come in 1936 to head the Nationalist forces in the Spanish Civil
War, was outmaneuvered by the French. So, in 1956, putting the
best possible face on a tactical defeat, Franco invited the Sultan of
Morocco to Madrid and joined the French, who had granted independence to French Morocco, in giving up Spanish claims to Morocco.
Spain did, however, retain two coastal towns, Ceuta and Melilla,
which had been in Spanish hands since the Middle Ages, and a coastal
enclave known as Ifni.

Ifni generated a setback in the rapidly developing friendship
between the United States and Spain when, in 1957, it was attacked
by Moroccan irregulars and almost overrun. The Spanish military
forces requested approval of their American counterparts to use
American-made military equipment to put down the attack. Much to
the dismay of the Spaniards, the request was denied. With help from
the French forces still in Africa, the Moroccans were defeated.
However, the American refusal has been used by Spanish critics of
the pact as additional evidence that the U.S.-Spanish bases agreement was onesided. The critics conveniently overlook the fact that
ten years later, in 1967, Spain ceded the territory to Morocco in
order to please the United Nations decolonization committee whose
blessing it sought in the Gibraltar dispute.[31]

Although the Franco government might have looked askance at
the prospect of a new and untried independent state of Morocco on
its southern flank, the change improved Spain's bargaining position
in its expanding relationship with the United States. By the time the
Spanish bases were operational for U.S. planes in the late 1950s,
the Americans had received notice to vacate their bases in Morocco.
This meant that the Strategic Air Command's Sixteenth Air Force,
previously with half of its strength in Morocco and half in Spain,
would be centered in Spain. Thus, U.S. dependence on Spain was
raised considerably.

Northern Europe

Relations with France understandably have always been accorded
high priority by the Spanish government. Traditionally France has

been Spain's third biggest export market for commodities and manufactures, and a large job market for Spain's unemployed work force.
France in the early 1960s supported Spain's early effort to join the
European Common Market and found an increasing Spanish market
for French technology and armaments. Once the Algerian War was
over, political relations between France and Spain steadily improved.
Each side had to take pains to avoid having the other's political refu-
gees intervene in the domestic affairs of their home countries. Sometimes serious violence was threatened, as in the case of French OAS
(Organisation de l'Armée Secrete) members who settled near Valencia,
Spain, and Spanish Basque (ETA) activists who moved just across the
border to the province of Gascony. However, the top officials of both
governments found it mutually beneficial to keep relations between
Spain and France on an even keel.[32]

Spain's greatest detractors in Western Europe were the Belgian,
Danish, and Norwegian governments, due primarily to the strength
of the Socialist and Labor parties in those countries. In addition,
Denmark and Norway, and to some extent the Netherlands, were
expressing Protestant opposition to Franco's Catholicism. Spain's
ties with Sweden were much more limited than ties with the others,
and of less importance in the context of Europe. While Switzerland's
role of an international banking center was valuable to Spain, given
the unique dual role of Spanish banks, it was not an important factor
as Spain emerged from isolation to rejoin Europe.[33]

The United States would have been pleased to see Spain admitted
to NATO and the Common Market, but it deliberately kept a low pro-
file in the belief that excessive advocacy could have backfired. In
making the connection with Spain, the United States had played its
trump card. It had little or no leverage left with its other European
allies who, after 1953, got whatever benefits could be reaped from
the U.S.-Spanish connection without the cost of closer ties with
Franco.

Spain's only real ally in Europe was, of course, Portugal. The
two nations had much in common, starting with their contiguous
position on the Iberian peninsula, and their commitment to Iberian
unity.[34] Both were ruled by iron-fisted dictators, Salazar in Portugal
and Franco in Spain. Salazar had aided Franco during the Spanish
Civil War, and then had stuck by him when most others had ostracized
him. Both countries had strategic advantages which were important
for the defense of the West. Portugal parlayed its assets, notably the
Azores, into membership in NATO where it espoused the cause of
Spain, but to no avail. The countries had their differences but kept
them in low key. It was ironic that Portugal, the junior partner on
the Iberian Peninsula, not only was admitted to NATO, but later was
a founding member of the Free Trade Association. For Spain, the

same reasons that drew it close to Portugal were barriers to its close association with the rest of Europe:

1. the destruction of the Spanish Republic in the civil war;
2. Spain's ties with the Axis powers in World War II; and
3. the personality and politics of General Franco.

Hispanic America

Spanish links with the Western Hemisphere were forged in the crucible of history. Wherever one looks—the Caribbean, South America, Central America, North America—one finds the stamp of Spain, its people, its language, its culture, and its religion. Yet the presence of Spain in Hispanic America has not resulted in the pervasive Spanish influence there that one, knowing the history of both regions, might have expected. There is, to be sure, understanding and mutual appreciation at the cultural level; but this does not translate into reciprocal trade or political support. During the days of Spain's greatest distress following World War II when it was economically prostrate and politically ostracized, Argentina alone helped Spain with loans for the purchase of wheat. It is ironic that Mexico, the one Hispanic American nation that never recognized the Franco government, maintained substantial commercial ties with Spain throughout his long dictatorship. It is equally ironic that Spain never stopped trading with Castro's Cuba, even after the United States imposed its embargo on that country in 1961. The Spanish government's emphasis on its cultural ties with the nations of the Americas was primarily through its Institute of Hispanic-American Culture which was housed in an impressive building near the University of Madrid.[35]

Two factors contributed to the relatively low-key Spanish official relations with Hispanic America during the first two decades after World War II. The first one was the clearcut failure of the Franco initiative to pull Latin America out of the Allied and U.S. orbit through the Hispanidad program in the war years. Brazil (with closest ties to Portugal) in fact fought in the Italian campaign, and Mexico had sent a squadron of planes to fight in the closing phase of the Pacific war. These nations, therefore, did not overlook Franco Spain's early leaning toward the Axis. The second factor was the cohesion of the American republics in the euphoric period after the chartering of the Organization of American States (OAS) in 1948 and continuing into the 1960s on the momentum of the Alliance for Progress.

The United States, after the end of World War II, did not view Spain as its rival in Hispanic America. Indeed, it recognized the profound cultural ties that linked the Hispanic world together. Certainly after the Pact of Madrid was signed, the United States believed

that Spain and Hispanic America could build strong economic relationships that would redound to the benefit of all three areas. That challenge is still open.

In retrospect, it is clear that the Latin American nations,
regardless of their cultural heritage, have been advancing steadily
toward independence in the fullest sense of the term. Concomitantly,
they have been changing the tone and the substance of their relations
with both Spain and the United States. By expressed preference they
are emerging from the cultural hegemony of Spain and the other
former colonial powers just as they are emerging from the political
and economic hegemony of the United States. Whether Spain and the
United States can profit from each other's experience in Latin America remains to be seen.

THE CONNECTION PAYS OFF: THE ECONOMIC
LIBERALIZATION MEASURES OF 1959

While the U.S. direct economic support to the Spanish economy
in the late 1950s and early 1960s was significant, no doubt much more
important to Spain was what the country got from the West in the
realm of political-economic ideas in the same period. Isolated, over-
regulated, and highly sensitive to economic security in the early
1950s, Spain encountered through its U.S. connection, and through
the contacts with Europe to which it led, a fresh introduction to the
case for liberal capitalism and free-market oriented economic policies which in the end was compelling. The adoption of important
liberalizing measures in Spain as part of the stabilization program
of the late 1950s laid the foundation for the remarkable progress of
the mid-1960s to mid-1970s decade which is sometimes referred to
as Spain's "economic miracle."

The causal relationship between the association with the United
States and Spain's economic liberalization measures of 1959 cannot,
of course, be exactly documented, but the course of events is clear.
Following the Second World War, the United States had made itself
a champion of liberal capitalistic ideas through the long reach of
its foreign policy. From its position of unassailable military and
economic dominance the United States had pressed on other nations
the theme that markets, not governments, provided the best means
of obtaining efficient resource allocation and the idea that monetary
and fiscal policies were the appropriate measures for securing stability in price levels and aggregate output. With populations of most
other industrialized countries in any case weary of wartime regulations and eager to regain personal freedoms along with prosperity,
the notion that governments should be disarmed of much of their

power to regulate specific production, consumption, and trade decisions, at the same time that governments were disarmed militarily,
had widespread appeal. Liberal ideas were the basis, therefore, of
the design of important postwar international institutions, such as
the International Monetary Fund, the World Bank, and the General
Agreement on Tariffs and Trade. These ideas were also impressed
by the United States on the Japanese in the form of that country's
postwar constitution and on the Western European nations in the
form of conditions on the 1947 British loan and in the form of goals
and conditions of the Marshall Plan. It was thus unavoidable that
Spain's U.S. connection would bring the Spanish face to face with
these proposals, and, indeed, make Spain's adherence to the institutions and symbolisms of a now unfashionable corporate state an
anchronism. Too strenuous a defense of outmoded corporatism would
only have served to remind both Spaniards and the outside world of
Spain's previous association with German National Socialism and
Italian Fascism. Given Spain's connection to the United States, and
given Franco's desire to gain the approval of the other nations rising
victorious from the ashes of the Second World War, it was inevitable
that economic liberalism would sooner or later encroach on Spain's
corporate state. The encroachment might, nevertheless, have come
much later had Spain's almost complete political isolation from
Europe and North America not been altered. The U.S. connection
implied opportunities for a new foreign policy for Spain, for traffic
in people between Spain and the United States, for the enlivenment
of foreign investment in Spain, and for the laying of foundations for
Spanish economic revival. These opportunities certainly were a
catalyst in accelerating Spain's acceptance of liberalizing economic
policies.

Advocates for liberalization, however, could only appear when
the time was ripe. Anderson[36] has described the period 1953-1955 in
Spain as one of pause in the process of economic problem identification in public discussion. Imports of U.S. foodstuffs against counterpart funds were helping then to stabilize the price of food, and there
was progress in investment in industry, public utilities, and transportation, even though deficient demand plagued production of some
consumer goods. Policy debate was quiet in this period.

Meanwhile, the U.S. economic assistance agreement nevertheless contained in its text some pledges by Spain to "general undertakings" that reflected chiefly American ideas. These commitments had been made by the Spanish government:

(b) To stabilize its currency, establish or maintain a valid
rate of exchange, balance its governmental budget as soon
as practicable, create or maintain internal financial

stability, and generally restore or maintain confidence in
its monetary system; and . . .

(e) To discourage cartel and monopolistic business practices and business arrangements which result in restricting production and increasing prices or which curtail
international trade, to encourage competition and productivity and to facilitate and stimulate the growth of international trade by reducing barriers which may hamper
such trade when the attainment of the agreed program
may be affected.[37]

For a country dedicated, as Spain had been up to that time, to
the achievement of a high degree of autarchy and protection of privilege, using an overvalued set of exchange rates, import quotas,
internal credit rationing, investment allocations, and price and other
controls, these were rather remarkable undertakings, and they may
well have not been taken terribly seriously by Spanish officials in the
haste of negotiations. Indeed, they may only have seemed to echo the
high sentiments expressed in many international documents of that
time. Certainly they were still for the most part beyond attainment
anywhere in Western Europe. Nonetheless, U.S. officials in Spain
took them seriously enough to see that their Spanish counterparts
did not forget them. The U.S. embassy mentioned them again and
again, aware that these phrases were certainly not empty ones for
the political process back at home.
    Among other idea patterns reaching Spain from the rest of the
world in the mid-1950s were those popularized by Raul Prebisch and
the United Nations Economic Commission for Latin America that
predicted futility and stagnation for less developed countries which
continued to depend on the more developed, industrialized countries
to be their markets and their source of supplies. Nations at the
"periphery," according to this theme, were doomed to being raw
material producing areas and doomed to deteriorating international
terms of trade unless they sought economic independence, alone or
in trading associations, from the dynamic countries at the world's
"center." In calling for trade protectionism and isolation, the doctrine provided a fresh rationale to some Spaniards for continuing the
autarchic policies by which Spain had been directed ever since the
1920s.
    Other political-economic themes stemmed from the democratic
socialist literature that had arisen in the 1920s and 1930s. In this
line of thought, poor economic performance in capitalist countries
was due to inequalities of economic opportunity, and capitalism was
a system driven by unattractive, possibly immoral, motivations.
Anathema to most of the ruling coalition in Spain, these ideas focused

more on changes in who would manage economic affairs in the country, and toward what ends, than on how the ends would be achieved since the Spanish socialists would presumably retain many of the interventionist methods, if not the actual institutions, of the corporate state economy, if they had their way.

But gaining ascendancy over these competing themes in Spain in the 1950s were the neoliberal ideas that emphasized the increase in social economic efficiency that could be achieved with increased freedom in individual decision making. This theme eschewed much of the polemic about income and wealth redistribution and focused on increasing the national product in which all could share. Striking achievements in initiating economic recovery from the war that were observable in Germany, France, and the Low Countries, in association with trade and payments liberalization programs and the dismantling of controls, provided a vivid testimonial in the 1950s to the power of a liberal approach.

Opportunity often comes with distress, and the opportunity for fundamental change in Spain came with the inflation and balance of payments crisis of 1957-1958. Fed by government budget deficits and by monetary growth that increased from a 7.2 percent per annum rate in 1953, to 11.7 percent in 1954, 14.8 percent in 1955, and 19.4 percent in 1956, inflation was acknowledged in 1954 and 1956 by government-decreed, across the board, public-sector wage increases. The rate of increase in Spanish consumer prices spurted from 1.0 percent in 1954 to 11.0 percent in 1957 and 13.5 percent in 1958. As a result of these financial disturbances, the balance of payments on current account worsened, and capital flight reached critical proportions in 1958. The nation's foreign exchange reserves fell from $73 million in 1954 to only $8 million in 1958, while gold holdings were halved, from 3.71 million troy ounces to 1.66 million.

The problems of Spain became, then, those which other countries were attacking with the still relatively new tools of macroeconomic policy, and increasing numbers of Spaniards were seeking to understand how these policies could be implemented in Spain. The implementation, however, was something for the experts in the "new economics," and increasingly their voices were heard.

In February 1957 new faces came to the chief economic ministries—Commerce and Hacienda (Treasury)—and to the Technical Secretariat-General of the Office of the Presidency. All three appointees, Alberto Ullastres at Commerce, Mariano Navarro Rubio at Hacienda, and Laureano Lopez Rodo at the Office of the Presidency, were identified with the Catholic lay order, Opus Dei, all were technically trained in economics or public administration, and all were neo-liberals. Three months earlier, the liberal-leaning Pedro Gual Villalbi had replaced Paris Eguilaz, a Falangist, as head of the National Economic Council and the Ministry for Economic Coordination.

The timing was propitious. In February 1957 the Treaty of Rome creating the European Economic Community was signed, launching a movement that would pull Spain more toward Western Europe and its style of political economy in the decades to come.

During 1957 Spain opened discussions with the OEEC, the IMF, and the World Bank which led to membership in these organizations in early 1958. The country's multiple foreign exchange rates were unified into a single rate although at this time a system of prior deposits and subsidies was retained. Credit restraints were imposed to brake the inflationary credit expansion, and steps were taken to improve the efficiency of business tax collections. In January 1959 a questionnaire directed by the cabinet to a variety of economically influential Spanish institutions found surprisingly little disagreement with proposals that Spain take a direction toward liberalization and association with European integration.

Early in 1959 Spanish officials welcomed delegations from the IMF and from the OEEC, and, because of keen interest in Spain in the 1958 stabilization program in France, invited one of that program's chief authors, Jacques Rueff, to Madrid. Out of these discussions and further internal planning came the decrees of July and August which were the backbone of Spain's 1959 stabilization plan.

The essence of that plan was in these actions:

1. An adjustment and freeing up of foreign exchange which amounted to a unification of the exchange rates at a somewhat devalued level of 60 pesetas per dollar.
2. Foreign trade liberalization, including a review of the tariff laws which resulted in adoption of the Brussels tariff nomenclature and a shift to universal use of ad valorem tariff rates, and "globalization" of what were formerly country-specific trade quotas with other OEEC countries.
3. Abolition of a number of public trading corporations responsible for importation and distribution of raw materials.
4. Adoption of measures to encourage foreign investment by increasing allowable foreign participation in projects and guaranteeing repatriability of some investment earnings.
5. External support to the peseta totaling $420 million, including $100 million in OEEC credits, $75 million from the IMF, $45 million from individual OEEC countries, $70 million from Chase Manhattan and First National City banks, $30 million from the U.S. Export-Import Bank, and $100 million in ongoing U.S. assistance programs, the last of which strengthened both the balance of payments and the government budget position.

6. A domestic attack on inflation, including reductions in public
   expenditures, tax increases, a freeze on wages, a ceiling on
   the use of bank credit by public sector agencies such as INI
   and the State Railways, and a release of the Bank of Spain
   from obligation to fund all state borrowings.
7. An antimonopoly law which, while not completed and promulgated
   until 1962, offered a restored position of favor to competitive
   behavior.
8. Tax reforms finally enacted in 1964, which increased the progres-
   sivity of direct taxation and simplified indirect taxation.

Not surprisingly, the immediate effect of the unilateral trade
liberalization and the inflation-dampening measures were a slowing,
rather than a quickening, of economic growth. Real GNP declined in
1959, and, in 1960, it was a bare one-half of 1 percent higher than
1958. The inflation of consumer prices, however, also slowed—to
less than 1 percent—and there was a marked turnaround in the
balance of payments. Not only did the merchandise trade balance
shift from a quarter of a billion dollar deficit to a small $41 million
surplus, but the groundwork was laid for the expansion of Spain's
tourist industry—a phenomenon of great importance for the years
ahead. Use of the loan package that had been assembled to support
the trade liberalization measures proved largely unnecessary, and
the credits were allowed to lapse in 1961.

The trek of northern European tourists to Spain's sun-filled
coasts was abetted by the 1959 currency depreciation and inflation
control measures but also by the steps toward payments liberalization
and economic recovery that were taking place in France, Germany,
Benelux, Scandinavia, and the United Kingdom. The number of tourists in Spain increased nearly 50 percent, from 4.2 to 6.1 million,
between 1959 and 1960, and Spanish earnings from tourism more
than doubled from $129 million to $297 million. These figures marked
the takeoff of a growth industry whose progress would not be checked
until the worldwide petroleum crisis of the mid-1970s.

Even as foreigners flocked to Spain's beaches, however, Spaniards also moved northward to find work. Unemployment and real
wage reductions associated with the disinflation in Spain combined
with labor shortages elsewhere in Western Europe to induce an
increase in Spanish emigration in 1960 of 60 percent relative to the
average for the preceding decade, and there was another doubling in
1961. The direction of Spanish emigration was sharply redirected
from Latin America toward destinations in Europe. The remittances
home of these expatriate workers made a growing contribution to
Spain's balance of payments.

The payoff of the new economic policies—fortunately supported by economic expansion elsewhere in Europe—began to appear in 1961, 1962, and 1963. Spanish GNP at 1975 prices finally leaped forward by 11.8 percent in 1961, and 9.3 and 8.8 percent, respectively, in 1962 and 1963. Inspired by this turnaround in the business climate and the new policy encouragements, foreign investors increased their annual commitments in Spain from $15 to $226 million between 1960 and 1961, and such investment averaged $178 million in the next two years. The flood of foreign capital to Spain, which would reach a rate of $5 billion a year within twenty years, was under way.

Price inflation unfortunately resumed with the acceleration of economic activity, and the balance of trade moved again to deficit. The trade deficits of 1961, 1962, and future years, however, now could be financed by ever-growing earnings from tourism, remittances from Spaniards working abroad, and capital inflows. Freed of at least a few of the shackles on their endeavors at home and abroad, Spaniards did not hesitate to exploit their new economic opportunities.

FROM COOPERATION TO COLLABORATION

During the early days of its new relationship with Spain, the United States, at least in Washington, portrayed its policy as a practical one and nothing more. This treatment, however, unavoidably changed with time. It was impossible to carry out a program of military cooperation with the Spanish armed forces, which were the main prop under Franco, without the appearance, and indeed the fact, of political collaboration with the Franco government. It was not long before the most prominent figures in Washington supplied visible evidence of that collaboration.

Secretary of State John Foster Dulles visited Madrid on November 1, 1955, en route home to Washington after a conference in Geneva on Southeast Asia. The Madrid visit was scheduled on short notice and was only a brief stopover for Dulles to call on Franco and have lunch with the Foreign Minister, but the impact was electric in Spain. It was also a signal to the rest of the world, notably America's NATO allies, of the esteem the United States accorded Spain. Two years later, on December 20, 1957, Dulles started what was to become customary for American Secretaries of State by stopping off again in Madrid to report to General Franco what had transpired at the most recent NATO Council meeting in Paris. Dulles' comments after the meeting with Franco made clear the upgraded relationship of Spain:

> I told him . . . of the basic policies and the strategies
> that were being followed. I felt that General Franco, by
> the contribution that his Government was making to the
> defense of Europe, had clearly entitled himself to that
> kind of information.[38]

Both Spain and the United States recognized the Pact of Madrid to be an alternative to Spain's participation in NATO. Both governments had recognized in 1953 that unanimous acceptance of Spain for NATO membership, as is required by the Alliance charter, was not possible. The Dulles visit in 1957 came at a time when Spain wanted very much to apply to NATO and expected the United States to take the lead in its behalf. Both the U.S. executive branch and the Congress, however, concluded in 1957 that applying pressure on NATO members to accept Spain would be counterproductive, so Spain had no alternative but to accept that verdict and wait almost 25 years— during which time the Spanish people themselves came to express ambivalence.

President Eisenhower visited Madrid on December 21-22, 1959, where he received a hearty welcome from General Franco and the people who lined the streets of the Spanish capital. There has been considerable speculation as to why the president chose to visit Madrid since that city was not included in the original schedule. It was not a case of persuading Eisenhower to go there. Eisenhower was willing to demonstrate Spain's importance to the United States. There were problems of finding time for the visit in an overflowing schedule and of perfecting every detail of presidential security and of communication. General Franco's remarks at the dinner honoring the American president were revealing:

> It is the first time that a President of the United States
> has come to Spain, and Providence has chosen this to
> occur at a time when our relations are reaching a point
> of maturity and understanding. . . . It is a motive of
> satisfaction for us, who see in the Agreements of 1953
> not only a circumstantial instrument of limited political
> cooperation, but a step further along the road of friend-
> ship for the two nations. . . .[39]

President Eisenhower caught the public eye when, on departing Madrid, he gave General Franco two abrazos (formal embraces).[40] The joint communique issued by the two chiefs of state on December 22, 1959, emphasized the "gratifying progress" that had been made in the "implementation of the economic and defense agreements of 1953."[41]

Even as General Franco was euphoric over the attention given him by President Eisenhower, however, the first breaches appeared in the wall of support which Spain had been receiving in the U.S. Congress. Notwithstanding the demise of Senator McCarran, Spain had received for a time enough congressional support to get special attention in appropriations; no member now, however, had McCarran's tenacity and sheer gall. One outspoken critic of Franco Spain in the late 1950s was a young Representative from Portland, Oregon, Charles Porter, who first attracted attention by criticizing the Trujillo dictatorship in the Dominican Republic and then lambasting Franco. In 1959, Porter made a long speech in the House providing a rationale for denying aid to Spain. Among his comments were:

> First. Franco was morally and actually on the Axis side in World War II. . . .

> Third. Even though our aid to Franco Spain amounts to almost $2 billion, Franco's policy has been to hide the extent and importance of this aid. He claims that current Spanish inflation is caused by the construction of American bases. . . .

> Seventh. We have no binding assurances that we will be able to use our military installations on Spanish soil in case of war. [42]

Porter does not seem to have been taken too seriously by his colleagues, and he was not returned to the Congress after his second term. A new and more formidable opponent of special consideration for Spain emerged soon thereafter, however, in the person of Senator Fulbright, later to become chairman of the Foreign Relations Committee in the Senate. Under sharp questioning from Senator Bridges of New Hampshire, who was now the strongest voice for Spain in the Senate, Fulbright let go with both barrels:

> As much as we admire and respect the Spanish people, I do not consider them to be the closest allies of this country over the years . . . . [To earmark funds for Spain] will tie the hand of the Administration. It will leave the Administration no room in which to negotiate with the Spanish Government . . . . There were some very special circumstances surrounding the origin of this program, going back to the days of the late lamented Senator from Nevada, with which we are all familiar. I do not want to get into that, but I do not think there is any justification for singling out one country and saying

that our country must give that country this money regardless of what are the conditions.[43]

Fulbright did not win his point, but public attention had now been drawn to the unique preferential treatment accorded Spain. Representatives of the Spanish government, which had endured far worse, did not give much attention to the new sounds of criticism in the U.S. Congress, and the Spanish public hardly knew about it since the press was controlled. The Spaniards in any case could take consolation, if they needed it, in continuing to receive annual funding, tagged for Spain, in excess of administration request.

The period from 1953 to 1959 could be described as the honeymoon of the U.S.-Spanish relationship. The program of economic cooperation had virtually transformed Spain, and had provided a threshold for Spain to reenter the Western community of nations. If the mood of the American Congress was changing, Spain could now anticipate commercial loans and foreign private investment instead of government aid on concessional terms. The fact that Spain seemed to be ready for that transition was a reflection of the fact that foundations had been well laid.

NOTES

1. Note Pursuant to the Second Paragraph of Article III of the Defense Agreement dated 27 September 1953.

In case of evident Communist aggression which threatens the security of the West, United States forces may make use of the areas and facilities situated in Spanish territory as bases for action against military objectives, in such manner as may be necessary for the defense of the West, provided that, when this situation arises, both countries communicate to each other, with the maximum urgency, their information and intentions.

In other cases of emergency or of threat of aggression to the security of the West, the timing and manner of utilization of the areas and facilities situated in Spanish territory would be the subject of urgent consultation between both Governments, and will be determined in the light of circumstances of the situation which had developed.

A. Viñas et al., Foreign Commercial Policy in Spain (1931-1975), Banco Exterior de Espana, 1979.

2. ABC, June 27, 1981, Antonio Garrigues, "The Spanish-North American Agreements."

3. Whitaker, Spain and Defense of the West, p. 60.

4. Testimony of Stewart H. Van Dyke, Regional Director, ICA,

in Mutual Security Appropriations for 1959, hearings before the Senate Committee on Appropriations, 85th Congress, Second Session, July 14, 1958.

5. Benjamin Welles, Spain, the Gentle Anarchy (New York: Praeger, 1965), p. 291.

6. Weeks, unpublished doctoral dissertation.

7. Whitaker, Spain and Defense of the West, p. 66.

8. Welles, Spain, the Gentle Anarchy, p. 291.

9. Rubottom, who was Deputy Director and then Director, USOM, Madrid, was fully committed to the idea of a Combined Economic Mission. Later, when Assistant Secretary of State for Inter-American Affairs in the Department of State, he insisted on having a Combined Economic Mission in Brazil, at that time the most important mission in Latin America.

10. See U.S. State Department Press Release 519, dated September 26, 1953, in The Department of State Bulletin, October 5, 1953, pp. 435-36.

11. Angel Viñas, "American Assistance to Spain: The Pact of Madrid, 1953-1963" (mimeographed, undated), p. 15 and footnote 15.

12. Rubottom viewed the film while stationed in Madrid.

13. A ten-year loan, for example, of $1 million at 5 percent, when the market rate of interest (and marginal social efficiency of investment) is 10 percent, is equivalent to a gift of $50,000 a year for ten years. This has a present value, when discounted at 10 percent, of $307,228. The loan, then, is worth more to the borrower than a grant of any amount less than $307,228. When, however, a loan or grant is "tied" in any way that restricts its use, the value of the loan or grant is reduced by the difference in the value of the use that is specified and that of the use that would have been preferred. All of the U.S. aid to Spain, loan and grant, was tied in some way or another.

14. Price level changes are not accounted for in the calculation.

15. This is the free market rate at that time.

16. Per capita income in Cadiz Province was still only 71 percent of that of Spain as a whole in 1971; in Sevilla it was 74 percent, in Murcia 74 percent, and in La Coruna 75 percent.

17. See OECD, Salient Features of Development Policy in Spain (Paris, 1973), p. 24.

18. See Ramón Tamames, Introducción a la economía española (Madrid: Alianza Editorial, 1980), pp. 388-89.

19. OECD, Technical Assistance and the Economic Development of Spain (Paris, 1967), p. 39.

20. Ibid., p. 25.

21. Ministerio de Commercio estimates of Spain's balance of payments, reported in Estadisticas Basicas de España, 1900-1970 (Madrid: Confederacion Española de Cajas de Ahorros), p. 301.

22. J. M. Alverez de Eulate, "Política de Financiación Exterior," in Luis Gamir (coordinador), Política Económica de España, vol. 1, Introducción, Instrumentes, 4th ed. (Madrid: Alianza Editorial, 1980), p. 161.

23. Weeks, unpublished dissertation, p. 144.

24. Here one should recall that the Spanish base construction program had not even started.

25. Townsend Hoopes, "Overseas Bases in American Strategy," Foreign Affairs, Fall, 1958.

26. Stephen S. Kaplan, "American Military Bases in Spain," Public Policy, Fall, 1974, p. 97.

27. Ibid., p. 101.

28. Ibid., pp. 96, 98, 107.

29. Arnold Hottinger, Spain in Transition: Franco's Regime (Beverly Hills, Calif.: Sage Policy Paper, 1974), p. 15.

30. Ibid.

31. Ibid., p. 16.

32. Ibid., p. 18.

33. Whitaker, Spain and Defense of the West, p. 298.

34. Hottinger, Spain in Transition, p. 61.

35. Whitaker, Spain and Defense of the West, p. 30.

36. Charles W. Anderson, The Political Economy of Modern Spain (Madison: University of Wisconsin Press, 1970), pp. 89-92.

37. Article II, Economic Aid Agreement. See "Agreements Concluded with Spain," The Department of State Bulletin, October 5, 1953, p. 437.

38. U.S. Department of State, American Foreign Policy: Current Documents, 1957 (Washington: Government Printing Office), pp. 617-18.

39. New York Times, December 23, 1959.

40. Ibid.

41. Ibid.

42. Snowcroft, Congress and Foreign Policy, p. 287.

43. Ibid.

3

The Maturing Relationship

Improved economic conditions were clearly visible in Spain by the end of the 1950s. Food shelves were stocked; there was dependable electric power to light cities and drive industry; transport was modernized; and there were jobs for those who wanted them. In its external relations, Spain had gained admission to all major international organizations except GATT (the General Agreement on Tariffs and Trade), and that would come in 1963. Still, only with the United States did Spain have a relationship of mutual respect and friendship, and the keystone of that relationship was an executive agreement which had to be renewed in 1963. Consequently, in 1960 and 1961 both parties were reviewing their situation as a prelude to re-negotiation of the agreement.

For the United States, Secretary of State Herter, in his testimony before the Congress in 1960, put it plainly but unenthusiastically: "In Spain we have military facilities of critical importance to us. The provision of a reasonable measure of help to Spain in dealing with its very real economic problems is not an undue measure of reciprocity."[1] In Congress Spain's special treatment continued under attack. Robert Dole, then a young representative from Kansas, offered an amendment to the authorizing legislation during the 1960 session which would require that "countries receiving assistance under this act shall guarantee to their people freedom of speech, freedom of religion, and freedom of the press." While defeated, the text of the amendment reflected something in the conscience of Americans deep in the heartland of the country.

Spain's leaders were, of course, equally outspoken in appraising the U.S.-Spanish relationship. Some spokesmen pointed out that, notwithstanding the obvious benefits to Spain of the program of economic

77

cooperation, one had to understand that the agreements had altered Spain's traditional neutrality and made the country more vulnerable to nuclear attack by the Soviets. General Franco himself publicly called attention to this in a speech at Burgos on October 1, 1961, first acknowledging the "steadfastness of our policy in the Agreement with America," but then warning that his armed forces needed new equipment to "correspond to the new situation."[2] The "new situation" clearly referred to a danger to Spanish cities from possible Soviet nuclear attack. Spain's Foreign Minister, as reported earlier, had already made this point while on a visit to Washington.

Spaniards were also beginning to voice their opinions regarding the terms of the economic agreement. A colonel in the Army Supply Corps, Angel Baldrich, in June 1957, wrote that while Spain was helping to defend the free world, its "economic assistance" from the United States was just enough to pay the cost of the land expropriated for the bases so that this could hardly be called compensation for its contribution to the defense effort.[3]

For the Franco government and for outspoken Spanish citizens, a careful measurement of the "balance and economic effects of North American assistance" was no mere intellectual exercise. It was an appraisal of Spain's fundamental choices. It was also part of a process that could influence the annual negotiations with the United States out of which came the dollar amount of defense support and related programs. In reviewing the congressional appropriations for the first decade of those programs, one must conclude that the Spanish negotiators used the process successfully, although they might not always have gotten as much as they sought.

Today's scholars find it easy to deprecate the accomplishments of the past. They don't fully sense the pressures that were being exerted on the actors of the time, and they have the benefit of archives to reveal negotiating positions, fallback positions, and "final" positions. In fact, it seems reasonable to characterize the American and Spanish negotiating postures of the early 1960s as efforts to build a pragmatic, workable arrangement rather than an unrealistic utopia. If either side pushed too hard, the American-Spanish connection might have severed just when it was beginning to produce its fruit. Both parties had to be sensitive to accusations that either had intervened in the internal affairs of the other.

One must be careful, too, not to view history too impatiently. The Spanish economic stabilization program illustrates this point. In less than a decade Spain moved through a stage of underdevelopment to one of "takeoff" and, finally, to the status of a modern industrial nation. Moreover, it can be argued that economic liberalization actually set the stage for political liberalization in the decade after Franco died. Yet some of today's critics assert that America's role in this experience was too little, too late, and a prop for Franco. There is no doubt that the process could have been carried out differently, but whether it could have been done better or faster is debatable.

RENEWAL OF AGREEMENTS

In examining the record of the discussions and negotiations leading to the renewal of the base agreements in 1963, three points are worthy of note:

1. There was less political sensitivity in the United States in the early 1960s, as compared with the late 1950s, to having a working relationship with the Franco government; in fact, the United States left no doubt that it desired to renew the agreements.
2. Spain sought to up the ante to the United States for the bases, and, even though it was not successful, that effort was an indication of the higher premium that Spain was to place on its assets in the future, and the fact that some influential sectors were dissatisfied with the U.S. connection.
3. The decisive factor in the successful conclusion of the re-negotiations was a role of a single individual, Antonio Garrigues, the Spanish ambassador to the United States; his personal relationship with President Kennedy, and his courage in dealing with General Franco were instrumental in the breakthrough.

The most dramatic description of the negotiations leading to a renewal of the base agreements is that in Benjamin Welles' book Spain—The Gentle Anarchy, published in 1965. Another valuable source of information regarding the negotiations is the unpublished doctoral dissertation by Stanley B. Weeks cited earlier.

The opening move leading to the 1963 negotiations was the presentation to the United States of a "grossly inflated" request for $250 million in U.S. military equipment in June 1961. The head of JUSMAG in Madrid, Major General Joseph Caldara, USAF, reportedly did everything possible to get the Spanish military to trim the request, which originally totaled $500 million! The request got no response from Washington, which tactic undoubtedly caused General Franco eventually to revise his approach.

When the formal negotiations actually began, the mood of the two parties was not conducive to a favorable outcome. The Spanish government started by advising the United States that it wanted a re-negotiation of the 1953 agreements instead of an automatic extension of them. Meanwhile, the Pentagon misread the Spanish attitude and attempted to negotiate the same kind of "offset" arrangement with Spain that it had with most of its other European allies. The "offset" required that Spain agree to purchase $85 million worth of U.S. weapons for each of the following three years as an offset to the outflow of gold in the United States. This "poorly timed and poorly prepared"[4] move was rejected quickly by the Spanish government.

The United States apparently did not take the Spanish rejection seriously, and decided to send the Deputy Secretary of Defense, Roswell Gilpatric, to Madrid. The Spaniards were capable of playing their own tough negotiating game, so they simply advised the American government that the cabinet ministers whom Gilpatric desired to meet with would be away from the capital on a hunting trip with Franco.[5] This meant the cancellation of Gilpatric's intended trip.

By March 1963 the two governments were stymied in their attempts to re-negotiate the base agreements. Both sides seemed to have miscalculated, the Spaniards placing too high a price on their demands, and the Americans underestimating the Spanish resolve to obtain a more favorable deal. However, time was not running in favor of Spain. The House Foreign Affairs Committee issued the Clay Report on Foreign Aid on March 20, 1963. For the first time it became clear that Spain could no longer expect the Congress to prescribe, irrespective of the recommendation of the Executive Branch, an amount of financial assistance for Spain that reflected the Spanish view. In fact, the Clay Report criticized U.S. aid to Spain as being "excessive."[6]

In the State Department, the traditional reserve toward Spain prevailed, with the Assistant Secretary of State for European Affairs, William Tyler, seemingly more concerned with the solidarity of the NATO Alliance than with the renewal of the Spanish base agreements. In addition, Ambassador Woodward, the American envoy in Spain, was taking a reserved position toward the renewal of the agreements, conveying his impression that Spain needed the U.S. presence perhaps more than the United States needed the bases.

As is already clear, most of these tactics were negotiating postures. The United States wanted to keep the bases active, and Spain knew that. Secretary of State Rusk visited Spain in 1961, carrying on the tradition set by Secretary Dulles before him. (Rusk told Rubottom in 1982 that there never was any doubt in the Kennedy administration of the importance of the Spanish bases.) What apparently was lacking was a unified and clearcut policy within the Executive Branch of the U.S. government as to how best to deal with the Spanish demands. Suddenly a negotiating catalyst appeared in the person of the Spanish ambassador to the United States, Antonio Garrigues, who had been in the United States since July 1962.

Garrigues was a prominent international lawyer in Spain who had represented many American firms. That his appointment was a surprise is an understatement since Garrigues had served in the Spanish Republic, before the civil war, as an official in the Ministry of Justice. He was known to be a liberal monarchist. The Garrigues presence in the United States was adroitly timed by General Franco because Garrigues had a personal tie to President Kennedy.

In retrospect, it seems clear that President Kennedy's personal involvement in the decision to renew the agreements with Spain in 1963 grew out of his respect for Garrigues. In 1939, Garrigues and his American-born wife, both devout Catholics and part of the Franco underground, were living in Madrid when it was under seige by Republican forces. Joseph P. Kennedy, Jr., a young man of 24 in 1939, was working for his father who was the American ambassador in London. Young Kennedy had written an honors thesis at Harvard the previous year entitled "Intervention in Spain," in which he stated his view that Franco was no worse than the Republican government which by that time had fallen under Soviet domination. In pursuit of first-hand information and experience, Kennedy traveled to Madrid in the spring of 1939 just as the city was being encircled by the Franco forces, and was on the verge of final takeover. Madrid was undergoing a blood bath, with Republicans and Communists turning on each other and both groups hunting down Franco sympathizers. Kennedy heard about Garrigues and his wife, and searched them out in order to get their unique appraisal of what was happening in Madrid. One day, Kennedy, Garrigues, and two Spanish friends were driving in Madrid when an armed Republican unit stopped them. When they were all lined up at gunpoint and asked for identification papers, young Kennedy produced his American diplomatic passport, which so impressed the militia men that they let all four men proceed.

Garrigues never again saw Joseph Kennedy, Jr., who was killed in World War II, but the story of the incident was widely known in the Kennedy family. When Garrigues presented his credentials to President Kennedy in 1962, they discussed the incident involving the president's older brother many years before in Madrid. One can deduce that this personal link between President Kennedy and Ambassador Garrigues contributed significantly to the renewal of the U.S.- Spanish base agreements in 1963 on terms that would meet the needs of both governments.

In the actual negotiations, Garrigues held his fire until March 1963. Then, with only six months remaining until the agreements would terminate, Garrigues called on President Kennedy. The president reportedly told Garrigues that the United States desired to continue its ties with Spain and that he, as president, would undertake "to help meet Spain's needs" if Spain would "recognize the political facts of life. "[7] With that high level commitment, Garrigues returned to Madrid and persuaded both Franco and Foreign Minister Castiella to give him full negotiating authority.

Garrigues knew, of course, that Spain would not get the amount of military aid it had asked for earlier. Instead he decided to seek a stronger and closer political relationship with the United States. According to Welles, the ambassador studied the texts of all U.S. treaty commitments then in effect, and chose as a model the U.S. treaty with Japan which called for periodic military "consultation. "[8] During the months of July and August, Ambassador Garrigues carried on rapid fire discussions with the Under Secretary of State for Political Affairs, Alexis Johnson, who was favorably disposed toward the new Spanish initiative. With Johnson's informal concurrence, Garrigues returned to Spain and obtained Franco's personal agreement to accept the U.S. proposition even though several of the Franco advisers seriously questioned the new arrangement.

Garrigues arranged for Foreign Minister Castiella, who was in New York for the U.N. General Assembly meeting, to meet with Secretary of State Rusk on September 26, 1963, the exact date of the signing of the agreements ten years before. The other details pertaining to the economic and military assistance quickly fell into place and the two principals, Rusk and Castiella, signed the agreement with hours to spare. According to one source, Secretary Rusk turned to Air Force Chief of Staff General Curtis LeMay and told him "your colleagues have helped to no small degree to make this Agreement a reality. "[9]

As in the case of any successful negotiation, there doubtless was plenty of credit to go around. Yet one would have to agree with Benjamin Welles that the success of the 1963 renewal negotiations was due principally to the efforts of Ambassador Garrigues in developing the interest and the goodwill of President Kennedy who, in turn, brought his influence to bear on the American negotiators in the Department of State. It is understandable that the Spanish government subsequently awarded Garrigues the Grand Cross of Carlos III for his role in the 1963 negotiations.[10]

Terms of the 1963 Agreements

The 1963 Defense Agreement was a renewal for five years, that is, to 1968. Foreign Minister Castiella and Secretary of State Rusk issued a joint statement underlining the importance of the continuing cooperation between the two nations. There were two significant new points in this declaration. First, the United States linked its agreement with Spain to European defense by declaring that the defense agreements of Spain and the United States "form a part of the security arrangements for the Atlantic and Mediterranean areas." Second, and even more important, the joint declaration declared that a "threat to either country would be a matter of common concern to both countries, and each country would take such action as it may consider appropriate within the framework of its constitutional procedures."

Since this expanded commitment on the part of the United States was to be the focus of considerable debate in the Congress, the actual text should be examined in greater detail. One standard appropriate for comparison would be Article 5 of the North Atlantic Treaty which states that:

> The parties agree that an armed attack against one or more of them . . . shall be considered an attack against them all, and . . . if such an armed attack occurs, each of them . . . will assist the Party or Parties so attacked by taking forthwith . . . such action as it deems necessary . . . .[11]

Obviously the American commitment to Spain was less broad than the commitments mutually assumed by the NATO partners.

But the new agreement did not end with the joint declaration. The United States and Spain also exchanged diplomatic notes establishing a Joint Consultative Committee on Defense Matters in Madrid. The committee was scheduled to meet monthly, involving the head of the U.S. military mission in Spain and the Spanish counterparts, to consider "military matters of mutual concern, so as to develop and improve through continuing military cooperation the security and effectiveness of jointly utilized facilities in Spain."

The United States agreed to grant Spain $100 million in military assistance, and Spain agreed to purchase $50 million of U.S. arms as an "offset." As expected, Spain obtained no economic grant aid by the renewal but was offered $100 million in Export-Import Bank loans. Of great significance to the United States, that country got a separately granted permit to base a squadron of Polaris submarines in Rota beginning in late 1963. Once again, the U.S.-Spanish connection worked to provide both parties with their essential requirements with neither side getting all that it wanted. The combination of personality and pragmatism had produced a deal.

Reaction to the Renewal

The New York Times was of the opinion that in real terms Franco had gotten "nothing" by the renewal.[12] On the other hand,

the Washington Post said that "the shrewd Franco had gotten all he
wanted"—"a new status as a partner" and "a virtual ally" of the
United States, as well as a "new degree of international prestige."[13]
It was the Economist of London that took the greatest amusement
from the renewal, comparing the negotiations to "an American soap
opera where the principals hurled corn flakes at one another in the
opening sequence, but are safely back in each others' arms in time
for the last commercial."[14]

The Spanish press considered the 1963 renewal to be an "alliance" with the United States.[15] Obviously, the Franco government
was pleased with the outcome of the negotiations, the best indicator
being the recognition which it accorded to Ambassador Garrigues.

The negotiations ended with relatively good feelings on the part
of both parties. Yet, to careful observers, there were some warning
signals for the future. Spain was getting more and more insistent on
having additional aid and additional recognition of its importance.
The U.S. Congress, on the other hand, would no longer be literally
the handmaiden of Spain's request for assistance; any additional
American commitments to Spain would come under closer and closer
scrutiny, especially as U.S. involvement in Vietnam heightened.

SHIFTING POLITICAL CLIMATE: 1963-1970

The Connection Under Stress

Until the mid-1960s, both parties to the connection continued
to put it to constructive use. In 1964, the National Aeronautics and
Space Administration (NASA) concluded an arrangement for tracking
stations in Spain which gave that country a significant role in the
U.S. space program.[16] In February 1965, Spain obtained a $24 mil-
lion loan from the Export-Import Bank with which to acquire from
American companies its first nuclear power plant.[17]

Nevertheless, serious problems were soon to arise which
would affect relations between the two nations, as well as the pros-
pects for renewal of the connection in 1968. The following is a brief
outline of those problems:

Spanish Trade with Castro's Cuba

In 1961 the United States had placed an embargo on its trade
with Cuba. Following that action, the United States began to urge
Spain to join in the embargo, referring to Article 6 of the 1953 Mutual
Defense Agreement, which pledged Spain's cooperation with the United
States" in taking measures designed to control trade with nations

which threaten the maintenance of world peace." In the spring of
1964, the Johnson administration announced that American aid would
be suspended to certain nations, including Spain, which traded with
Cuba. [18] This action provoked a strong negative reaction in Spain,
whose trade with Cuba amounted to only $12 million annually. Shortly
afterward, because of protests at home and abroad, the United States
cancelled its threatened action, but the incident left a residue of
bitterness.

The Palomares Incident

On January 17, 1966, a Strategic Air Command B-52 bomber
collided over southeastern Spain with a KC-135 refueling plane,
releasing four unarmed bombs. Three of them landed near a Spanish
fishing village, Palomares, and were recovered within a few hours
after the accident. The fourth bomb was not recovered until April 7,
1966—eighty days after the accident. Nobody was injured in the crash
or contaminated by radioactivity, but the Spanish government insisted
that all future flights of American planes carrying nuclear bombs be
banned from flying over Spain. The United States promptly agreed
to the demand. (It announced in 1970 that flights over Spain with
nuclear weapons had never been resumed.)[19] For the first time the
Spanish government was required to defend before its own people
the presence of U.S. forces in Spain under the Pact of Madrid. Even
with a controlled press, this was not an easy task, and so the concept
of fear was planted. This incident unquestionably contributed to the
enormous increase in Spain's asking price for the 1968 base renewal
a few years later.

The Gibraltar Incident

In January of 1968, a large contingent of the U.S. Sixth Fleet,
including the carrier flagship, paid a visit to Gibraltar. Since
Gibraltar is the most sensitive issue in Spain's international relations,
everyone from General Franco to the man in the street reacted furi-
ously to the U.S. action. Even the Spanish military sector publicly
criticized the United States.[20] The Spanish government immediately
sent a formal protest to the United States and suggested that it would
consider banning U.S. ships from Spanish harbors, a threat which
was never carried out. Still, the visit was a major irritant.

U.S. Investment Restrictions

On January 1, 1968, the Johnson administration announced
restrictive measures on American foreign investment, including
Spain. This was a blow to Spain's development plans because during

the decade 1960-1970 the United States had become the largest foreign
investor in that country. The fact that Spain was classified with
the "industrialized nations of Western Europe" against which the investment action was taken, was small compensation for a step which
was seen as damaging to the Spanish economy.

ANOTHER RENEWAL

Notwithstanding the above problems which affected the political,
economic, and military climates in both countries, the parties to the
connection moved ahead with preparation for the 1968 renewal negotiations. The incidents focused attention on the increased price which
Spain would demand for the renewal of the agreements: upgrading the
agreements to treaty status (this was quietly dropped when it was
found to coincide with the position of Spain's opponents in the American Congress), sharply increased military assistance, a reduction
to the American military personnel in Spain, Spanish exemption from
overseas investment restrictions and even support on the Gibraltar
issue. And, as should have been expected, the above Spanish demands
played directly into the hands of the most outspoken critics of the
Franco regime in the United States.

Meanwhile, the United States was reassessing its need for the
bases in Spain. The Chairman of the Joint Chiefs of Staff, General
Earle Wheeler, publicly outlined the rationale for the bases at the
April 1969 hearings before Senator Fulbright's Foreign Relations
Subcommittee on U.S. Security Commitments and Agreements
Abroad.[21] The military reasons for keeping the bases was due to
their value in maintaining the conventional force presence of the
United States in the Southern Europe-Mediterranean area. In addition,
a joint State-Defense Department document submitted to the Foreign
Relations Subcommittee noted:

> The Soviet Mediterranean Naval Squadron, which first
> began operations in 1963, has been expanding steadily
> over the past several years . . . it could threaten the
> strategic balance upon which countries on the littoral,
> such as Spain have relied . . . the support which the
> Spanish bases supplied to the American presence in the
> Mediterranean area, however, adds to the strength of
> our forces . . . .[22]

General Wheeler also cited "the French military withdrawal from
NATO" and noted that with "the restriction on overflights of France

and Morocco, our current overflight rights in Spain take on added value. "[23] He concluded:

> It is the judgement of the Department of Defense that
> the availability of the Spanish base complex and oper-
> ating rights will continue to be militarily of great
> importance to the United States during the next five
> years. [24]

Negotiations 1968

In early 1968 the Spanish government formally requested negotiations on the future of the agreements, stating that an automatic
five-year extension was not desired. The responsibility for developing an American position for the negotiations was assigned to an
Inter-Departmental Group chaired by the Assistant Secretary of
State for European Affairs. It in turn reported to the Senior Depart-
mental Group which was responsible for the top level coordination of
foreign policy and was chaired by the Under Secretary of State. In
his unpublished dissertation, Weeks makes a strong point that the
Secretary of State effectively "lost control" of the negotiations and
permitted them to be taken over by U.S. military officials who were
primarily interested in the bases.

The role of the American military was undoubtedly upgraded
by the decision of the Spanish government to send a senior general to
Washington in June 1968 who, of course, met with a U.S. military
team. The general was authorized to present a military aid request
of $1 billion "as quid pro quo in connection with the extension of the
Defense Agreement. "[25] As should be expected in the case of exorbi-
tant demands, the United States did not take seriously the Spanish
opening bid. In September 1968 it offered Spain $140 million in mili-
tary grant aid. [26] The Spaniards promptly responded with their
"final" request for $700 million in military aid "plus a defense agree-
ment guaranteeing American assistance in case of foreign aggression. "[27] With the two parties almost half a billion dollars apart, the
Spanish government on September 26, 1968, the anniversary date of
the agreements, formally invoked the complicated termination procedure of the original 1953 defense agreement. This provided the
two parties with an additional six months "consultative period" (until
March 26, 1969) to reach agreement and then, failing such agreement, gave the United States one year to get out of Spain. As if to
emphasize its feelings, the Spanish government made "an official
declaration" on the same day saying that it would "welcome the removal" of the Torrejón Air Base, the one situated close to Madrid. [28]

The atmosphere was hardly conducive to a prompt and successful renewal of the agreements. The situation was made more difficult
by the announcement of President Johnson that he would not seek re-
election in 1968. This made Secretary of State Rusk a "lame duck"
official and, in effect, forced the American military officials to take
an even more prominent role in the negotiations. As it turned out,
those developments eventually had a negative impact on the Spanish
negotiating position. Instead of being able to capitalize on the surprisingly candid statement of the U.S. need for the Spanish bases,
the Spanish government, by delaying its actions, was eventually
forced to contend with an increasingly vocal opposition in the U.S.
Congress to any putative American commitment in Spain, let alone
any possible upgrading of that commitment.

As so frequently happens in the United States, the ongoing negotiations between the military officials, normally conducted in low
key and without benefit of daily press review, suddenly exploded into
major headlines. The U.S.-Spanish connection was no longer considered on its own merits, or even in the context of European defense.
It was caught in the web of Vietnam, just like other international
questions.

The Public Demands a Pullback

With President Johnson in a "lame duck" role following the
election in November 1968, the Chairman of the Joint Chiefs of Staff,
General Earle Wheeler, U.S. Army, went to Spain as the head U.S.
negotiator. While there, he sent a memorandum to his Spanish counterpart, General Diez Alegría, stating "by the presence of U.S. forces
in Spain, the U.S. gives Spain a far more visible and credible security
guarantee than any written document."[29] While that statement obviously was trying to explain to Spain why a treaty arrangement with
the United States was unnecessary, it still was interpreted by the
Congress and the American public, already wary of excessive military commitments because of the Vietnam situation, as going too far.

To make matters worse, the deputy commander of NATO
forces and of U.S. forces in Europe, General David Burchinal, to
whom Wheeler had delegated his negotiating responsibilities, on
December 6, 1968, signed a document of "agreed views" with the
Spanish military leaders, which, he stated in a preparatory note,
"must constitute" the basis for future negotiations.[30] Burchinal also
wrote that the United States was obligated to defend Western Europe
of "which Spain is an integral part." The press immediately interpreted the latter statement as an extension of the NATO defense
guarantee to Spain without congressional approval.[31]

In early 1969 there was a wide flurry of negative publicity regarding the Wheeler and Burchinal statements. The Spanish government protested, claiming that the publicity stemmed from "a deliberate leak aimed at sabotaging the talks."[32] Both sides cooled off after the Spanish government had received assurances from the United States that there had been no intention to create difficulties. General Burchinal, in turn, signed a new statement with his Spanish military counterparts, in which the controversial statements noted above were deleted.

An Interim Agreement Is Reached

With the Nixon administration in the saddle, the National Security Council, headed by Henry Kissinger, became responsible for the review of U.S. policy toward Spain.[33] Apparently it did not take long to confirm the conclusions made by the military the year before than Spanish bases remain "of great importance to the United States." This was to be the underlying rationale for the American negotiating position in the somewhat turbulent months ahead.

The Spanish government decided to play for time. On the day the pact would have expired, March 26, Foreign Minister Castiella called on President Nixon and Kissinger, following which the two governments announced "agreement in principle" on a renewal of five years. This was a move to avoid placing Spain in the position of having to serve notice on the United States to get off the bases within one year, and also it was an umbrella to cover the continuance of the negotiations. Their differences had narrowed on the all-important subject of the amount of military assistance—Spain insisting on $300 million, the United States offering $175 million—but the issue remained.

While the delaying tactic gave the Spanish government time to get acquainted with the new administration in Washington, the renewed spotlight, following announcement of the extension, augmented the criticism in the Congress and in the press of doing business with the Franco government, and also evoked the comment: "The seemingly unending war in Vietnam has produced a distinct distaste for taking on any more obligations."[34]

Spain's main political obstacle was in the Senate. Just as that nation had found its "deliverer," some two decades earlier, in Senator McCarran, it now found its nemesis in Senator Fulbright. And Fulbright was in the position to make his opposition count. As chairman of the Foreign Relations Committee he not only had a key voice in authorizing, or withholding, foreign assistance funds, but also his committee decided whether or not to confirm ambassadorial appointments. He signaled his intent during the hearings which resulted in the confirmation of Robert Hill as President Nixon's appointee as the new ambassador to Spain on April 22, 1969.[35] Hill's nomination never was in actual danger because he had made many friends in the Congress when he had served as Assistant Secretary of State for Congressional Relations more than ten years earlier.

What Fulbright announced was his intention to attempt to force the administration to negotiate any new bases agreement with Spain in the form of a treaty that would require Senate approval. It was ironic that Spain itself had sought treaty status for its American bases agreements only a few years earlier. Now the issue was being raised in the American Congress, a coordinate branch of the government, in a way that could be adverse to the Spanish interest because it was (1) linked to the embarrassing question of "doing business with the Franco dictatorship," and (2) caught up in the anti-Vietnam psychosis which was spreading like a virus in the United States. One newspaper wondered "thy the Foreign Relations Committee had never previously felt the necessity of examining this agreement . . . ."[36] The answer clearly could be found in the national frustration over Vietnam which now was manifesting itself in the Congress.

Another Interim Agreement—Until September 26, 1971

The U.S.-Spanish connection clearly was in trouble. Leaders in both governments who in a showdown would admit that the Pact of Madrid had been mutually beneficial, faced at least three sets of problems.

The constitutional question on the U.S. side was imminent with Senator Fulbright powerfully situated to carry out his threat to require that the agreements with Spain be upgraded to treaty status. The international question was the one that gripped the American public. Just how important were these Spanish bases with the cold war receding, another Israeli-Arab war inflaming the Middle East, and American involvement in Vietnam so unpopular that President Johnson, practically speaking, was forced from office? The third question was that of the U.S. perception of Spanish negotiating tactics. Spain's demands for economic assistance had been excessive and, even though their sights had been lowered, the tactical blunder had not been forgotten. Even worse, Spain in 1968 had tried for a brief time to play the neutralist card, threatening through Foreign Minister Castiella to turn to the Soviet Union for accommodation and possible support. This tactic, too, had boomeranged.

In the light of the above problems, Spanish Foreign Minister Castiella came back to Washington in May 1969 with an offer to

extend the interim agreement for another year, in effect, nullifying
the agreement in principle for a five-year extension reached only
two months before. The Nixon administration promptly accepted the
Spanish offer, so on June 20, 1969, the agreements were extended
two years from the original September 16, 1968, expiration date.
It is interesting to note, in light of the original Spanish request, that
the United States agreed to provide $50 million in military aid to
Spain, as well as $25 million in Export-Import Bank loans to pur-
chase arms.[37]

The new interim agreement seemed to please both sides. The
Spanish Foreign Minister had been under attack for pushing his demands too far, so he could claim credit for a new arrangement with
the American government, and also announce the deactivation of one
of the least used air bases at Morón.[38] With rare unanimity, all
sides in the United States seemed pleased. The Executive Branch
was happy because the Spanish bases had been retained. Senator
Fulbright was happy because by signing only an interim agreement,
it seemed "a step toward liquidation of the [Spanish] military bases.
. . ."[39] The Senate Foreign Relations Committee approved the
$50 million aid request for Spain, notwithstanding earlier objections.

It would be misleading, however, to assume that the temporary
aura of goodwill regarding the Pact of Madrid was anything more
than that. The showdown on the constitutional question in the United
States was only a year away.

Franco "Flexibility" and Nixon Finesse—
The Renewal of August 6, 1970

Both governments now seemed to realize that they could no
longer afford to engage in futile, time-consuming bargaining before
getting down to serious negotiation. Franco was making important
moves that would have a long-term impact on U.S.-Spanish relations.
In the summer of 1969, he named Bourbon Prince Juan Carlos, the
grandson of Spain's last king, to be his successor as head of state.
In October of 1969, Franco changed his entire cabinet for a variety
of reasons, replacing the hardline Castiella with a new young Foreign
Minister, Gregorio Lopez Bravo. One of the stated guidelines of
Franco's new cabinet was that Spain should have "flexibility" in the
conduct of its foreign relations.[40] The first expression of the new
"flexibility" was Lopez Bravo's visit to Moscow in January 1970 to
explore the possibility of consular and commercial agreements with
the Soviet Union, although the visit did not result in the resumption
of full diplomatic relations. Shortly afterward, Spain signed a $90
million purchase agreement with France to acquire 30 Mirage 3-E

jets. These moves obviously caught the attention of the United States and, in effect, strengthened the hand of the group which gave priority to a renewal of the Spanish bases agreement.

Meanwhile, the world was not standing still as witnessed by (1) the growing Russian presence in the Mediterranean, (2) the bitterness following the 1967 Israeli-Arab war, and (3) the expulsion of the United States from Wheelus Air Base in Libya. The Libyan action, in fact, caused the United States to ask for permission from Spain to reactivate the Zaragoza base in Spain,[41] which was granted.

Even with such trump cards as the situations described above, Spain carefully avoided overreaching in the 1970 negotiations. Lopez Bravo surprised his American counterparts by requesting "scientific, educational, social and economic aid," instead of the usual large amount of military aid.[42] The new Spanish request received prompt approval by the American government and a tentative signing date was set for May 1970 when Secretary of State William Rogers planned to visit Madrid.

But such quick success was not to be. The negotiating schedule was derailed by the U.S.-South Vietnamese invasion of Cambodia in early May 1970. This caused such an uproar in the United States as to make vulnerable any international involvement, even the U.S.-Spanish agreements, so the two governments decided to pull back from the earlier timetable.

In the meantime, Spain continued to flirt with France and, in fact, signed a limited military agreement with that country for joint maneuvers and arms manufacture in June 1970.[43] This action precipitated a decision by the United States to go ahead with a five year "Agreement of Friendship and Cooperation" with Spain, this being announced in mid-July. Senator Fulbright immediately demanded that the planned agreements be submitted to the Senate in treaty form.[44] President Nixon, not to be outdone, arranged a ceremony at the State Department in Washington on August 6, 1970, at which time Secretary Rogers and Foreign Minister Lopez Bravo signed the new agreement.[45]

This agreement contained nine chapters including the following topics: general cooperation, educational and cultural cooperation, scientific and technical cooperation, cooperation on environmental and urban development problems, agricultural cooperation, economic cooperation, and cooperation with respect to public information.

As usual, the most vital part of the agreement was in Chapter VIII termed "Cooperation for Defense," which stated that the United States and Spain

—within the framework of their Constitutional processes, and to the extent feasible and appropriate, will make compatible their respective defense policies in areas of mutual interest and will grant each other reciprocal defense support.

The chapter also provided that "each government support the defense system of the other," and obligated the United States to contribute, after obtaining funds from the Congress, $60 million in military grants to modernize Spanish defense industries. Of the amount, $35 million would be combined with $15 million in Spanish funds to build a joint aircraft warning network. The remaining $25 million in grants was earmarked for providing the Spanish army with various kinds of heavy equipment. The United States also authorized $120 million in Export-Import Bank credits to purchase 36 F-4C Phantom jets, and to lend Spain indefinitely 16 naval vessels.

Very important from the Spanish viewpoint was the fact that the bases were designated "Spanish military installations" instead of joint U.S.-Spanish bases. The United States gave up its control of the petroleum pipeline, which had cost $25 million to build in the previous decade, as well as any claim to the residual value of the bases in Spain. The estimated total cost of the new agreement to the United States over a period of five years was approximately $300 million. [46]

Senator Fulbright was forced to admit that President Nixon had finessed him by having the agreements signed before he could take action of any kind on the Senate floor, other than his earlier stated demands that the agreement be submitted in the form of a treaty. In effect, the United States had committed the full prestige of the nation toward the fulfillment of the agreement once it was signed. [47] But the chairman of the Foreign Relations Committee was not quite finished with the hard game that he was playing. He demanded and got Under Secretary of State Johnson and Deputy Defense Secretary Packard to testify before the Senate Foreign Relations Committee on August 26. Johnson's statement said that the treaty was "not appropriate" since the new agreement made no commitment to Spain's defense; he denied that there was any "secret annex" to the agreement committing the United States to Spain's defense; and finally acknowledged that "as far as the military aspects of the agreement are concerned, it is substantially a continuation of the arrangements that existed since 1953." [48] Johnson also knocked down any supposition that the agreement contained some new Spanish link to NATO, but then added that the NATO allies had been consulted and were "very pleased" that a new agreement with Spain had been reached. [49]

Since Senator Fulbright was unable to attend the hearing described above due to the death of a family member, the meeting was somewhat anticlimactic. Nevertheless, Senator Fulbright later took public credit for having reduced the scale of the American commitment to Spain in the 1970 renewal of the agreements. The best example of the Senator's influence was a public statement by Under Secretary Johnson that the United States had insisted in its negotiations with the Spanish government that part of the language of the 1963 Joint Declaration—"A threat to either country would be a matter of common concern"—be deleted from the new agreement "in recognition of the concern expressed by some members" of the Senate Foreign Relations Committee. [50]

In the final analysis, President Nixon's "victory" over the Senate might have been a pyhrric one. Three years later, in 1973, the Congress was to pass the War Powers Act, which would restrict not only President Nixon but all future executives in the exercise of their prerogatives as president. Certainly that was a high price to pay, although it is not the function of the writers of this paper to make a judgment on the merits of such a basic question.

One thing loomed clear after the 1970 renewal of the agreements. The Pact of Madrid continued to be strategically important to both parties. General Franco was willing to shake up his entire government in order to produce a "flexible" approach that would enable him more easily to reach agreement with the United States. President Nixon was willing to confront directly the Senate of the United States, and its powerful chairman of the Foreign Relations Committee, in order to be certain that the United States could continue its pragmatic connection with the Franco government.

THE SPANISH ECONOMY IN THE 1960s
AND EARLY 1970s

Spain's increased confidence in its negotiations with the United States in 1963, 1968, and 1971, was probably due in part to the performance of the Spanish economy which was transforming a backward and primarily agricultural nation into a newly industrialized state. Much of the change corresponded to the period when efforts were made to focus Spanish economic policy making in the National Development Plans of 1963, 1968, and 1972. An argument can be made, nonetheless, that the Spanish economic achievements of the 1960s owe more to the country's "opening to the West" in the 1950s than to the process of planning in the 1960s.

Economic ideas have their fashions, as do ideas about so many things, and in the decades of the 1950s and 1960s economic planning for growth was in fashion. The Dutch, the French, the Swedes, the British, and governments in scores of less developed countries established planning offices to ponder statistical series and project the course of selected sectors of their national economies. Since plan fulfillment was not mandated, at least for the private sectors of these economies, the approach was termed "indicative" to distinguish it from the more thorough planning and control methods of socialist nations. Its rationale was that by proposing a rate of growth for the economy as a whole, announcing targets for government activity including public investment, and exploring implications of these changes for various sectors of the economy, the plan increased the likelihood that the growth target selected would be achieved. The approach reflected an absence of faith in the power of competitive markets to identify growth bottlenecks, to rank priorities, and to motivate investment activities. The World Bank, emphasizing the imperfection of markets and an alleged scarcity of entrepreneurship in less developed countries, was an important patron of such planning.

Sadly, planning advocates did not foresee the problems that would arise from the politicization of an increased number of economic decisions. And they could not anticipate the degree to which national planning models would be driven off course by the worldwide inflation of the 1970s and especially by the widespread changes in supplies of energy, labor, and savings. By the end of the 1970s disenchantment with planning was such that in many countries, including the United States and Spain, the idea that governments should limit their role in economic affairs was regaining supremacy in political discourse.

The First Development Plan

Spain's introduction to formal planning came in the early 1960s. Even before recovery from the deflationary effects of the 1959 stabilization plan had appeared, the Opus Dei economics ministers in Madrid created an office of planning commissioner in the Office of the Presidency and issued an invitation to the World Bank to send a mission to Spain "to assist the Spanish Administration in the preparation of a long-term development program designed to expand and modernize the Spanish economy . . . ."[51] The excellent mission report, widely read in Spain, emphasized the possibilities for growth in the country through the reallocation of labor and capital from lower to higher productivity uses. The bank mission especially stressed what could be achieved through recission of (a) the Spanish laws favoring public enterprises, (b) the investment controls inhibiting the mobility of capital and risk taking, (c) the restrictions of imports and foreign investment, (d) the restraints on bank competition and bank loan selection, and (e) the job tenure rules limiting the termination of employees by employers. The report called for the rationalization of much of the government policy making apparatus to secure better coordination among the parts and to subject the whole to greater scrutiny.

The decree-law instituting Spain's first development plan was signed by General Franco on December 28, 1963.[52] It set a goal for the annual real growth rate in Spain's gross national product at 6 percent, a full percentage point higher than the bank mission's projection of 5 percent. The organization for planning that was provided for owed much to the planning system in France—just as the Spanish stabilization plan of 1959 had owed much to the French stabilization program of 1958. While the plan paid heed to the "need for a marked reduction of government activity in the various sectors of the economy,"[53] it tended, nonetheless, to rely more on explicit government activities to induce change than had the World Bank mission report, and this bias that opened the door for special interests to use political influence to maintain their existing protection from change continued while the execution of the first and subsequent plans took place. It is probably fair to say that the first plan was more candid than the World Bank report had been concerning the need to consolidate smaller enterprises into larger ones and to shift labor from poverty stricken agriculture to opportunities in manufacturing and services. The plan set quantitative targets for its terminal year, 1967, for the main aggregates: gross national product, imports, exports, private and public consumption, and gross capital formation. It also set specific goals for the labor force and its allocation and for the education, agriculture, fishing, energy, industry, and transportation sectors. A short chapter devoted to regional development played a role in slowing the concentration of Spain's population into a few metropolitan centers.

"Miraculous" Economic Growth

The performance of the Spanish economy in the decade 1961–1970 was extraordinary by any measure. The gross national product at 1964 prices almost doubled, from 862 to 1,588 billion pesetas between 1961 and 1970—an average annual growth rate of 7.5 percent which was the highest of all OECD countries except Japan. Resources were shifted from agriculture to manufacturing and services at a remarkable rate. Whereas the share of population employed in agriculture in 1960 was 41.7 percent, in 1969 it was only 30.2 percent; and whereas agriculture and forestry accounted for 22.7 percent of the gross national product (at current prices) in 1960, that share was down to 14.1 percent in 1969. Manufacturing on the other hand, expanded in real terms at an annual average rate of 9.5 percent,

1960-1969, and public utilities and construction grew at 10.8 and
9.7 percent rates. Services—including transport and communications,
commerce, financial services, and other services—grew even faster
so that by 1969 services accounted for 45 percent of GNP as compared to only 37.9 percent in 1960. Spain was "the fifth industrial
power in Europe" in 1972,[54] the industrial base having grown most
rapidly in the heavy industries, shipbuilding, chemicals, petroleum
refining, automobile production, steel, and cement.

Tourism was also an extraordinary growth industry in this
period. The number of foreign visitors converging on Spanish beaches
and historic sites grew nearly fourfold, from 5.5 million to 21.3
million annually, between 1961 and 1970, and by 1972 the figure was
31 million. The currency devaluations of 1959 and 1967 helped to
keep Spain one of the travel bargains of Europe.

In a reverse flow of persons, Spanish workers emigrated in
large numbers to other parts of Europe, actively encouraged by the
Spanish government throughout the 1960s. Spain's intent was presumably to increase the productivity of the emigrants, to induce
mechanization of Spanish farms, and to relieve unemployment in the
poorer provinces without adding to congestion in the Spanish metropolitan centers. Most of the workers went to Germany, France, and
Switzerland with expectations of staying less than two years. The
net number crossing the Pyrenees to the north totaled nearly half a
million during 1960-1965, before recession in central Europe forced
a temporary net return flow in 1966 and 1967. There were probably
1.1 million Spaniards employed outside Spain in Europe by 1970, and
remittances of these workers back to Spain contributed $1.9 billion
to the current account of Spain's balance of payments over the span
of years 1964-1970.

Attack on Regional Imbalance

Regional imbalances in Spain, which are perhaps greater than
in any other country in Europe with the possible exception of Italy,
were addressed in each of the three development plans. The first
plan, noting that populations of twelve southern and western provinces
had per capita incomes less than two-thirds the national norm, introduced a program of government subsidies to industrial firms locating
in selected "development poles," "promotion poles," or "industrial
polygons" (demarked geographical areas). La Coruña, Sevilla,
Valladolid, Zaragoza, Vigo, Burgos, and Huelva were selected as
poles in the first plan, and Granada, Cordoba, Oviedo, Logroño,
and Villagarcia de Aroso were added in the second. The Canary
Islands and Campo di Gibraltar—the area behind the contested rock—

had special development programs. Subsidies included official credit
at less than market rates, cash grants that could be as much as 20
percent of investment in a "promotion pole," a reduction of up to
75 percent of customs duties and border taxes on imported equipment, free depreciation, help with land acquisition, and exemption
from various local taxes, license fees, sales and capital transfer
taxes.[55] The government also invested heavily in improving the
transportation and health infrastructure of the pole areas. To be
eligible for the subsidies, firms, for their part, had to assure the
government of investments that would create specified numbers of
jobs and meet other conditions. An OECD Working Party in 1973
appraised the success of the Spanish regional development program
by saying that "there has been a strengthening and expansion of
medium-sized towns which has improved the spatial distribution of
industry [and secured] a spreading of technological progress and of
educational and social improvement . . . ."[56] The success of the
program was not such, however, as to warrant the creation of new
poles in the third development plan (1972-1975), and the earlier designated poles were terminated on a schedule in which the longest duration was ten years.

Foreign Trade

Spain's foreign trade in the 1960s reflected the transformation
that was occurring in the national economy. Exports of manufactures
and semimanufactures grew sevenfold in U.S. dollar terms during
the 1961-1970 decade (some 22 percent per annum), aided in the final
part of the period by the 1967 devaluation. Total exports of goods
more than tripled. Foremost, but by no means alone, among the
successful export industries were shipbuilding and shoes. Import
protection remained high (by European standards) both in nominal
and "effective" terms[57] but was reduced significantly by general
tariff cuts in 1963 and 1964 and by various exemptions allowed
selected producers through special programs. Theberge shows
nominal protection—consisting of customs duties plus border taxes—
falling from 18.7 to 15.5 percent between 1961 and 1970. He estimates that effective protection for import-competing industries
declined from 68 to 37 percent during 1961-1966; for non-import
competing industries the decline was from 288 to 72 percent; and for
all manufacturing it declined from 125 to 51 percent.[58] Commodity
imports more than quadrupled between 1964 and 1970 (from $1.1 bil-
lion to $4.7 billion), and the trade gap was kept manageable only by
growing receipts from the provision of "services" to foreigners,
especially tourism and repatriation of emigrant earnings.[59] The flow

of imports from the United States widened from $182 million to $580 million, but exports to the U.S. increased also from $59 million to $304 million, narrowing the bilateral trade gap in proportional terms although not in terms of absolute dollars.

Foreign Capital Sustains the Growth

The reductions in restrictions on foreign investment that accompanied the stabilization plan of 1959 and that were broadened in 1963 opened the gates to a flood of private corporate capital from abroad in the 1960s. At first it was largely American (45 percent U.S. as compared to 20 percent for the EEC in 1961-1962), but subsequently it was more equally spread (32 percent U.S. and 31 percent EEC in 1969), as a result of the U.S. restraints on capital outflows in the late 1960s. For the period 1960-1974 as a whole, more than one-third of such direct investment (34.8 percent) stemmed from the United States, and the remainder was largely Swiss (18.7 percent), German (11.8 percent), and British (11.3 percent). The investment flow, which averaged $150 million a year in 1965-1969, was directed chiefly to the Spanish chemical (including petroleum refining, tires, and fertilizer) industries, production of basic metals, electrical equipment, automobiles, processed foods, and other consumer goods. Alvarez de Eulate reproduces a 1970 Ministry of Industry list of the 100 leading industrial firms in Spain which indicates that foreign-based multinational firms participated in 50 of them, 16 of the foreign participants being U.S. [60]

Other forms in which foreign capital supported the Spanish growth in the 1960s were foreign loans to large scale public and private Spanish enterprises (averaging $130 million a year, 1966-1969), and foreign purchases of real estate in resort areas ($109 million in 1969). There was some sporadic borrowing by entities of the Spanish state. What is clear is that Spain's creditworthiness had become well established in the international capital market. Altogether, foreign sources were providing almost 10 percent of total gross investment in Spain in 1965, 1966, and 1967.

Preferential Agreement with the EEC

When Spain first applied for membership in the European Economic Community in 1962, the application made little progress, partly as a result of concern in EEC countries about absence of political freedoms in the Franco regime. Even in 1970, when a preferential trade agreement was signed, full membership for Spain was unacceptable. That agreement did provide, however, for a progressive reduction of trade barriers between the EEC and Spain over a period of six years. The EEC, for its part, was to reduce the common external tariff applied to Spanish industrial products generally by 60 percent over three years, although the average reduction on agricultural goods was only 17 percent. Spain, on the other hand, would reduce tariffs on EEC goods by about 27 percent by 1977—the concessions varying by specified commodity lists—and would also increase total quotas on EEC exports to Spain by 13 percent per annum. The result of the preferential agreement was that the share of Spanish exports directed to the EEC (including the United Kingdom, Ireland, and Denmark) grew slightly, from 46.4 percent to 47.8 percent, between 1970 and the 1973 onslaught of the petroleum crisis. The share, not surprisingly, declined thereafter because of the disturbance to trading patterns brought on by the manifold increase in the price of petroleum. The share of Spanish imports provided by the EEC similarly grew from 40.8 percent to 42.3 percent between 1970 and 1973 and then declined to 34.7 percent by 1975. As for Spain's trade with the United States, the share of Spanish exports going to the United States declined slightly in the pre-oil crisis period (14.1 percent to 13.8 percent), as did the share of Spanish imports coming from the United States (18.9 percent to 16.1 percent).

Appraisal: The Period of Rapid Growth

This vast transformation of Spain's economy that took place in the sixteen years between the stabilization plan of 1959 and the end of the Franco era is certainly woven out of threads initiated in the U.S.-Spanish relationship of the 1950s. History is a walk through time in which each step influences what can be achieved with the next. Spain's opening to the West with the 1953 Pact of Madrid resolved pressing economic problems in the 1950s, set in course a trend toward more liberal Spanish economic policies, and created opportunities for more productive relations with North America and the rest of Western Europe. Many of the building blocks of the 1960s economic progress followed this stimulus, and each reinforced the others—investment by multinational corporations, increases of productivity in agriculture and industry, expanding domestic saving and investment, growing exports of goods and tourist services, emigration, and Spain's association with the EEC. While Spain's rapid growth was financed chiefly through indigenous saving and investment, rather than through foreign capital, the indigenous capital formation was supported by the buoyancy the foreigners imparted to the economy. The investors from abroad brought to Spain not only financing for imports but a new breed of management, advanced technology, and connections to sales and distribution channels on foreign markets.

Various critics of the U.S.-Spain relationship have pointed to the risks and costs for one or the other country of the connection, and the risks and costs were real. Nonetheless, there were also returns from the relationship. For the United States, the returns took chiefly the somewhat nebulous form of an enhanced sense of national security; for Spain the long-run payoff was in measurable economic magnitudes as well as in less measurable but no doubt real progress toward responsible democracy.

The role which the indicative planning process in Spain played in the economic achievements will of course always remain debatable. The changes carried out under the plans of 1963, 1967, and 1972 certainly had positive influences, accelerating the movement of persons and capital toward particular uses through selective subsidies. The planned changes, however, also no doubt had negative influences. Some of the regional "poles" selected for development, for example, never "took off;" some of the agricultural consolidation efforts involved large expenditures with negligible effects on output; and the political pressures on the planning process may have prolonged rigid structures in the markets for labor, financial assets, and selected products in a way that slowed important adaptations relative to what would have happened without such intense government efforts at resource management.

Certainly Spain's great growth push began before the inauguration of the first plan. Coming out of the recession of 1960, real Spanish GNP expanded by 11.9 percent in 1961 and by 9.2 percent in 1962. From the inauguration of the first plan in 1963 through the rest of the decade the growth rate averaged only 6.5 percent. Furthermore, the conditions ripe for rapid economic development were largely put in place by the time of the economic stabilization program of 1959, before the start of the 1963 development plan. Price stability was restored in 1960-1961, and external payments were brought into balance. Measures demonstrating a welcome to foreign investment were put in place, and the nation's probable political stability was evidenced, for better or worse, by the internal and external support that flowed to the Franco regime after the U.S. agreements. Possible future alignment with the EEC could be seen by the end of the 1950s as a result of the U.S. role as broker between Spain and Western Europe, and as a result of Spain's entry into the OECD, the IMF, and the World Bank. A number of large U.S. firms moved quickly in 1960 and 1961 to establish their beachheads in an economy that appeared ready for rapid improvement. At least the initiation of Spain's "miracle," therefore, preceded the country's national plans.

At the beginning of the 1970s concern arose in Spain about the degree of external control that foreigners could exercise on the economy through their investments. Studies of particular industries showed high degrees of penetration by foreign-based multinational firms in sectors such as rubber, chemicals, electrical machinery, petroleum, paper, extractive industries, non-electrical machinery, transportation equipment, basic metals, and food processing.[61] One must remember in interpreting and using the penetration data, however, that development was taking place from a low base of industrial activity; as a consequence, where one or a few technologically advanced plants were added to an industry with a very low level of output, the new plants were bound to loom large in the industry for a time. To the extent that there was competition in the form of imports or domestic products which were very reasonable substitutes for the product in question, the foreign investors had few opportunities for economic exploitation. Furthermore, given that foreigners faced competition and were motivated by hope of profits, foreign investors' incentives were largely in consonance with Spanish efficiency objectives. Most important, before one criticizes too seriously the potentialities for influence in Spain that foreign investors might have had, the positive contributions that the investors made must be remembered. Foreign firms not only (1) financed facilities which raised the productivity of indigenous Spanish factors of production, they (2) demonstrated and taught new technology and management know-how to Spain, (3) added capital to the domestic tax base, and (4) in some cases restrained, by their competition, economic abuses being perpetrated by Spanish monopolists and holders of privilege whose positions were not easily assailable by other means.

NOTES

1. U.S., Congress, House, Committee on Appropriations, Mutual Security Appropriations for 1961 (and Related Agencies), Hearings before the Subcommittee on Foreign Operations Appropriations, 86th Congress, 2nd Session, 1960, p. 102.
2. ABC (Madrid), October 2, 1961.
3. Angel Baldrich, "Balance y Efectos Económicos de la Ayuda Norte Americana," Moneda y Credito, June 1957, p. 45.
4. Welles, Spain, The Gentle Anarchy, p. 299.
5. Ibid., p. 301.
6. Ibid., p. 302.
7. Ibid., p. 304.
8. Ibid., p. 305.
9. Max Gallo, Spain Under Franco, translated by Jean Stewart (London: George Allen and Unwin, 1973).

10. Ibid.

11. NATO Handbook (Brussels: NATO Information Service, February 1976), p. 10.

12. New York Times, September 27, 1963.

13. Welles, Spain, The Gentle Anarchy, p. 308.

14. "Lease Extended," Economist (London), October 5, 1963, p. 33.

15. Washington Post, October 6, 1963.

16. Eduardo Chamorro and Ignacio Fontes, Las Bases Norte Americanas en España (Barcelona: Editorial Euros, 1976), p. 143.

17. Ibid.

18. Welles, Spain, The Gentle Anarchy, p. 280.

19. U.S., Congress, Senate, Committee on Foreign Relations, Hearings on Spanish Base Agreements, 91st Congress, 2nd Session, August 6 and 26, 1970, p. 47.

20. Chamorro and Fontes, Las Bases Norte Americanas en España, p. 145.

21. Hearings, U.S. Security Agreements and Commitments Abroad, pp. 2303-2414.

22. Ibid., p. 2400.

23. Ibid., p. 2353.

24. Ibid.

25. Ibid., p. 2350.

26. Ibid.

27. Christian Science Monitor, November 20, 1968.

28. Ibid.

29. Hearings, U.S. Security Agreements and Commitments Abroad, p. 2356.

30. Washington Post, February 25, 1969.

31. Ibid.

32. New York Times, March 1, 1969.

33. Washington Post, April 22, 1969.

34. Christian Science Monitor, May 27, 1969.

35. Washington Post, April 22, 1969.

36. Ibid.

37. Washington Post, June 6, 1969.

38. Chamorro and Fontes, Las Bases Norte Americanas en España, p. 145.

39. Florida Times-Union (Jacksonville), June 6, 1969.

40. New York Times, October 29, 1969.

41. Hearings, U.S. Security Agreements and Commitments Abroad, p. 2398.

42. New York Times, April 15, 1970.

43. Christian Science Monitor, June 26, 1970, p. 5.

44. U.S., Congress, Senate, 91st Congress, 2nd Session, July 28, 1970, Congressional Record, pp. 12259-60.

45. New York Times, July 25, 1970.

46. New York Times, August 7, 1979.

47. Hearings on Spanish Base Agreement, p. 59.

48. Ibid., p. 18.

49. Ibid., p. 39.

50. Ibid., p. 12.

51. The mission's report was published in English as The Economic Development of Spain: Report of a Mission Organized by the International Bank for Reconstruction and Development at the Request of the Government of Spain (Baltimore: Johns Hopkins University Press, 1963). The objective of the mission cited in the text is from p. vii.

52. In English, the plan appeared as Economic and Social Development Program for Spain, 1964-1967, prepared by the Commissioner for Economic and Social Development Planning, Presidency of the Government of Spain (Baltimore: Johns Hopkins University Press, 1965).

53. Ibid., p. 16.

54. Harrison, Economic History of Modern Spain, pp. 163-64.

55. See James Theberge, "Spanish Industrial Development Policy in the Twentieth Century," in William T. Salisbury and James D. Theberge (eds.), Spain in the 1970s: Economics, Social Structure, Foreign Policy (New York: Praeger, 1976), pp. 14-19.

56. Organization for Economic Cooperation and Development, Salient Features of Regional Development Policy in Spain (Paris: OECD, 1973), p. 48.

57. Effective protection is a measure of the increase in value-added given to domestic producers by trade restrictions that may affect raw materials and other production inputs as well as the values of outputs.

58. James Theberge, "Spanish Industrial Development Policy in the Twentieth Century," pp. 22 and 25.

59. By 1972 tourism earnings and emigrant remittances covered more than half of Spain's import bill.

60. Alvarez de Eulate, "Política de financiación exterior," pp. 169-73.

61. There is a review of some of this literature in Alvarez de Eulate, "Política de financiación exterior," pp. 154-64.

4

The Seventies—
Spain in Transition

A GLANCE BACKWARD

Following the signature of the agreements in 1970, just as on similar occasions going back to 1953 when the Pact of Madrid was first signed, there was no time for euphoria. It must have seemed to the negotiators that the U.S.-Spanish connection had had to withstand every kind of adversity.

The two nations had never known each other well. Their only direct relationships had been marked by doubt and distrust at best, and outright hostility, even war at worst. When the original agreements were signed on September 26, 1953, Spain had overcome a strong cultural bias in the United States based on religion, a strong political bias based on the American perception of the harsh Franco dictatorship, and an historic economic bias based on American opposition to Spain's autarchic policies enforced by strict government controls. Indeed, at each step it had taken overwhelming support from the American military sector to balance the equation enough for the Spanish base agreements to be continued.

Spain had its problems, too. The most prominent members of the Catholic hierarchy were opposed to having large numbers of Americans take up residence in Spain. Most military officers were loathe to give up Spain's traditional neutrality. Spain's hard-line rightists feared an "invasion" of Americans reared in the practice of democratic freedom, while Spaniards on the left, the Socialists and Communists, were more than dubious about American "capitalist imperialism" and would also have preferred to keep the Americans out.

Yet every adversity had been overcome. Spain had achieved respectability, and most importantly, self-respect. It had been re-integrated into Western Europe. It had liberalized its economy and attained growth rates that were astonishing even to the most optimistic. It had opened its doors and become an attractive opportunity for the world's investors as well as one of the most popular tourist regions of the world. None of the expected problems had materialized as a result of the coming of American servicemen and their families.

Spaniards nevertheless had three gnawing concerns about their relations with the United States. First, they worried about the location of the air bases near Spain's largest cities, particularly the one at Torrejón, only fifteen miles from Madrid. Second, they began to wonder, especially as inflation fires began to burn, whether they had placed too low a price on the bases in terms of economic support. Third, Spain had not yet achieved that ultimate sign of respectability, admission to NATO and to the EEC.

The United States could help with the first and second problem, as subsequent negotiations in the 1970s were to reveal. The United States had tried, but could do nothing more to alleviate the third one. By then, it must have been clear to every Spaniard, including Franco himself, that admission to NATO and the EEC would have to wait until Franco's demise.

NEGOTIATION OF A "DECLARATION OF PRINCIPLES"

President Nixon paid a state visit to Spain on October 2, 1970, not long after the signing of the 1970 agreements. It is noteworthy that Presidents Eisenhower and Nixon, followed later by President Ford—all Republicans—visited Spain. No Democratic president did so until Carter went there in 1977—after Franco's death.

The question arises of how best to influence a nation. Certainly the United States was interested in the political evolution of Spain, and indeed, it was staking a great deal on Spain's becoming a constitutional monarchy with full democratic freedoms, once Franco was gone from the scene. President Nixon obviously felt that, by working with the government in place, he could best influence the events to come. In fairness, one could hardly quarrel with this judgment in the light of Spain's democratic evolution since the death of Franco in 1975. Presidential visits are, of course, symbolic and ritualistic. They do not deal with specific problems, of which Spain and the United States had their fair share.

One problem did arise in 1973, following the Arab-Israeli war, that threatened for a time the U.S.-Spanish mutual understanding.

Even though U.S. bases were not supposed to be used in support of aircraft en route to the Middle East, in fact air force tanker planes based in Spain were used to refuel F-4 Phantom jets being flown nonstop from the United States to Israel, and this was done without any specific notice to the Spanish government.[1]

The Spanish government protested this use of the bases and stated that "the sole function" of the bases was for use to meet a threat "against the security of the West" in accordance with the 1970 agreement.[2] Obviously Spain, with its long history of support for the Arabs and the only country in Western Europe never to have recognized Israel, did not associate "the security of the West" with the security of Israel. Following this incident, Spain made known its intentions to demand a mutual security treaty with the United States in place of the agreements of the past.

As for the United States, the events of October 1973 underlined the old question of Spanish limitations on U.S. use of the joint bases. It should be observed that the U.S.-NATO allies made even stronger protests over the use of their facilities by the United States to aid Israel, so Spain had good company. Spain, also, was careful to make its protest after the fact, rather than interfere with the use of the bases at the time the refueling was underway.

Secretary Kissinger visited Spain in December 1973 to explain that the United States regretted any misunderstanding that might have arisen during the Arab-Israeli war, and more importantly, to start exploratory discussions for the base negotiations which would have to begin in 1974. Secretary Kissinger met with the prime minister of the Franco government, Admiral Luis Carrero Blanco, and with Spain's new foreign minister, Laureano Lopez Rodó. Following their meeting on December 19, 1973, a joint communique was issued which stated that:

> Agreement was reached in principle to develop a Joint U.S.-Spanish Declaration of Principle. Both parties agreed that Spain is essential for the security of the West. They agreed as well that Spain must participate on a basis of equality with the other countries of the Atlantic area. . . .[3]

Although the U.S. offer to Spain fell short of a formal security treaty, as the Spanish government had earlier demanded, the above communique was widely interpreted as meaning that Spain was being given "equal to parallel status" to that of NATO allies.[4]

Sometimes the march of human events is stranger than fiction. This was the case in Spain, and those events were to have a profound impact on the U.S.-Spanish connection. A short time after Secretary

Kissinger left Madrid for Washington, Prime Minister Carrero Blanco was assassinated by a bomb set off under his car by members of the Basque terrorist group ETA.[5] It should be noted that Vice President Ford in his first official visit after assuming that office represented the United States at the funeral of the slain prime minister.

In retrospect, the assassination undoubtedly changed the direction of events that Spain would take in the years ahead. One news account observed that Franco "had expected the dour Admiral to keep Spain on a rightward course when he himself died and to make certain that his successor as Chief of State, Prince Juan Carlos, did not fall prey to liberal ideas."[6] Certainly the relatively successful attempts to democratize Spain which did occur following the death of Franco might have been more difficult, if not impossible, had Carrero Blanco survived as premier.

Franco named the former Interior Minister Carlos Arias to succeed Carrero Blanco. In a televised speech on February 12, 1974, Arias referred to the 1970 U.S.-Spanish Agreement of Friendship and Cooperation as a "treaty"—perhaps a deliberate slip to indicate his expectation for the future negotiations.[7]

Meanwhile, the United States and Spain began to negotiate the declaration of principles which had been announced back in December 1973. The head of the Spanish negotiating team was the new foreign minister, career diplomat Pedro Cortina. Apparently there was considerable discussion between the two governments as to whether the declaration should be "initialed" or formally signed. The Americans decided simply to initial the agreement, whether based on prescience or good fortune. At any rate, General Franco, already in declining health, entered a Madrid hospital a few days later, with the result that his temporarily designated head of state, Prince Juan Carlos, turned out to be the Spaniard to initial the declaration. This action was widely interpreted by outside observers as an indication that the United States intended to place its full support behind Prince Juan Carlos as its best hope of encouraging a peaceful transition from Franco to what was hoped would be a democratic post-Franco government in Spain.

The "Spanish-American Declaration of Principles" consisted of ten brief articles. Some of its more interesting provisions were these:

> Article I was a declaration that the United States and
> Spain considered that their cooperation since the year
> 1963 has been beneficial for the security of both countries,
> and that it has fortified the defense of the West with Spain

playing an important role, in this respect, in the zones of the Atlantic and of the Mediterranean. [8]

Article III, perhaps the most significant article of the Agreement from the standpoint of future U.S. policy toward Spain, reiterated the intent of the two countries to continue the existing cooperation based on a stable friendship, through the reciprocal support of their defensive efforts. . . . [9]

As ironic as were some of the declarations in the original Agreement of 1953 was the following from Article IV, in which the United States and Spain agreed that their cooperation had contributed to preserving the values, the ideals, and the aspirations that are based on the dignity and the liberty of the individual.

Article VII stated that a threat or attack on either of the two countries would affect both, and that each country would adopt that action which it considered appropriate within the framework of its constitutional processes. [10]

The last article mentioned above was very close to the language of the 1963 Joint Declaration and, although similarly vague, carried a strong suggestion of mutual defense responsibilities. This would have pleased the Spanish but might have created a problem with the American Congress except for one fact. The Congress was focusing all of its attention on President Nixon, who was in his last month of office, so the U.S.-Spanish declaration of principles got little notice in the American press.

SPAIN HELPED BY OUTSIDE EVENTS

That foreign relations cannot be conducted in a vacuum was never better demonstrated than in 1974 when an incredible chain of events occurred in Portugal, Cyprus, Turkey, and Greece, the sum total of which made the American bases in Spain, and U.S.-Spanish relations, more important to American security than before. It was as if the unpredictable had become predictable, with the only question being exactly where and when it would occur.

Portugal led the way. On April 25, 1974, the successor to long-time dictator Salazar, Caetano, was overthrown. Whatever hope that the United States might have had that Portugal would remain a dependable ally was soon dashed. The new regime in Portugal was highly unstable and turned sharply leftward, which tendency was to prevail for more than two years. The situation in Spain was hardly analogous to that in Portugal, which had fought long colonial wars in Africa, thus alienating from the political authorities many of the military officers who constituted the normal base of support to the regime. But, given Portugal's proximity to Spain, and the rapidly declining health of Franco, the Portuguese instability raised the priority of Spain in the eyes of the Americans.

In August 1974 there was an attempted coup against Cypriot leader Archbishop Makarios which prompted a Turkish invasion and subsequent occupation of more than half of Cyprus. The Cyprus crisis almost exactly coincided with the resignation of President Nixon; consequently the United States was hardly in a position to use whatever leverage it might have had in that drama. Later that year the U.S. Congress voted to withhold further U.S. military assistance to Turkey in an attempt to pressure Turkish withdrawal from Cyprus. The gesture failed completely and resulted only in the stiffening of Turkish policy toward Cyprus and forced the closing of many U.S. intelligence facilities in Turkey.

Greece was immediately caught up in the rush of events. The discredited right-wing military dictatorship in Greece was over-thrown shortly after the Turkish invasion of Cyprus. Although the new Greek premier, Karamanlis, was nominally partisan to the United States by virtue of his background, he responded to the public outcry in Greece by withdrawing Greek military forces from NATO and reducing the American presence in Greece.

The events described above, coupled with the growing Soviet presence in the Mediterranean Sea, revealed the strategic insecurity facing the United States on the southern flank of NATO. Within Spain itself, Franco had suffered a severe jolt at the end of 1974 with the assassination of Premier Carrero Blanco. Moreover, his illness early in that year, from which he partially recovered, evidenced to all that the end of the Franco rule was certainly at hand. The problem, and certainly the opportunity, which the outlook of Spain without Franco posed for the United States was stated well in a Washington Post editorial:

> It is hardly too soon for the United States to weigh how, during the post-Franco period, it can make known and make effective the American interest in Spain's long overdue transition to orderly democratic rule. [11]

As subsequent events were to show, the United States began to implement a carefully balanced policy toward Spain: on the one hand, it sought to stay close enough to Franco to obtain the cooperation necessary to maintain the Spanish bases which were more important than ever; and, on the other hand, it sought to develop close ties with potential leaders who would take over in Spain on Franco's demise and stall until a clearer perspective might come into view.

THE END OF RAPID ECONOMIC GROWTH

The years 1974 and 1975 brought momentous changes to Spain's economy. Unwise efforts to extend the long period of growth by demand expansion in 1971-1973 resulted in escalating inflation. Then the international petroleum crisis that followed the October 1973 selective embargo on petroleum sales by the Organization of Petroleum Exporting Countries severely impacted Spanish costs of production and the balance of payments. Following the assassination of Admiral Carrero Blanco in 1974, the Opus Dei technocrat ministers left the cabinet, and Spanish development planning came to an end.

These changes marked the end of Spain's twelve-year economic miracle. After vigorous expansion, at rates of 8.5 and 8.4 percent in 1972 and 1973, the Spanish economy slowed in the second half of 1974, and in 1975 it experienced GNP growth of barely 1.0 percent. Inflation, meanwhile, as measured by the consumer price index, soared from the already worrisome rate of 8.1 percent in 1972 to 15.7 percent in 1974 and then to 24.5 percent in 1977. The inflation was fed by a money supply growth that had swelled from 8.3 percent in 1970 to 26.2 percent in 1973; the rate of price increase was then kicked upward by the OPEC-enforced increase in energy costs and by wage costs. An index of wages jumped from 57.5 to 100 between 1973 and 1975 (the index based on 1975). While the climb in interest rates lagged behind the inflation in Spain, as it did elsewhere, Spanish stock share prices collapsed to only 43 percent of their 1973 level by the end of 1977. By 1975 Spain found itself hopelessly infected with the malaise which was worldwide and which came to be called in the Anglo-Saxon countries "stagflation."

THE McCLOSKEY-STABLER NEGOTIATIONS, 1974-1976

With the declaration of principles between the United States and Spain in place in 1974 serious negotiations toward renewal of the bases agreement began. In March of that year Secretary Kissinger announced that Robert McCloskey, ambassador-at-large, would head the American team negotiating with Spain. McCloskey had been the press spokesman at the end of the Johnson administration where he gained the respect of the press, and of important members of Congress by his honesty and professionalism.

In the case of any important negotiation, the American ambassador in the capital of the country concerned usually plays a very important role. Following an abortive effort to appoint a former Nixon aide, Peter Flanigan, as ambassador to Spain, President Ford, in December 1974, appointed career diplomat Wells Stabler, then Deputy Assistant Secretary of State for European Affairs, to be the U.S. ambassador to Spain. While McCloskey was the principal negotiator, commuting almost monthly between the United States and Spain for more than a year, Ambassador Stabler also contributed to the eventual successful outcome of the negotiations, receiving public credit from McCloskey for his extraordinary entree to the king and the senior ministers of the Spanish government. [12]

The chief Spanish negotiator was Juan José Rovira, who had been involved with the program of cooperation with the United States from the inception of the Pact of Madrid in 1953. No American could match his experience. He was counseled by other experienced Spanish diplomats, some of whose opinions are worthy of note here.

A former foreign minister, Castiella, still advocated a "hard-line" Spanish policy. [13] He also stated that U.S. presence in Spain constituted ". . . more a risk than a protection," and said that "the era of overseas military bases is over." [14]

Former Ambassador Antonio Garrigues, the one principally responsible for the 1963 renewal of the agreements, took a more sympathetic view of the U.S. role.

> We are dealing with a political negotiation, not military,
> not economic, not technical-cultural. Its basic aim is
> to obtain an improvement and an anchoring of the polit-
> ical relationship between the United States and Spain. [15]

He then alluded to a very sensitive point relating to the presence of nuclear weapons which, he said, "creates a problem of security for the Spanish people—as attested by Palomares—of the maximum gravity." [16]

Another important opinion was expressed publicly by the former Ambassador to Washington Jose Maria de Areilza, Count of Motrico. Areilza was one of four Spanish politicians who got in serious trouble with Franco for trying to deliver a memo to Secretary of State Rogers during the latter's visit to Madrid in 1970. The memo had simply noted that Spain's eventual membership in NATO depended on the abolition of authoritarian institutions, the establishment of political parties, and free elections. [17] Unpopular though that statement was with Franco, it was the simple truth and reflected

the views of most members of the American Congress, not to mention
the views of the European members of the NATO Alliance. His statement about the U.S. relationship when the new set of negotiations
began was especially meaningful since he was to become the first
foreign minister of post-Franco Spain, and he would eventually sign
the 1976 treaty with the United States.

> In the actual context of the world, dominated by two nuclear
> super powers, there is really slight margin for maneuver
> for a nation of middle size like Spain. Our geographic situ-
> ation makes even more limited the options for our own
> foreign policy. I personally believe that our national inter-
> ests of various sorts—military, economic, political and
> commercial—make advisable a deep understanding with
> the United States in the present situation. [18]

He also correctly forecast that the "climate in Congress" and the
"situation . . . of the executive" in the United States made a treaty
unlikely. [19]

The base-renewal negotiations were carried on at a steady pace
for a year, from late 1974 to late 1975. At first, the Spanish position
was to insist on treaty status for the ultimate agreements, but eventually this had to be dropped. At Spanish urging, the United States
pressed the NATO allies for a formal acknowledgment of the contribution of Franco Spain to NATO's defense, but this turned into an
embarrassment for Spain when the NATO allies replied in the negative. Doubtless that initiative was taken by the United States because
of the generally tough stance the Spaniards were taking in the negotiations, but it boomeranged on both parties.

President Ford's Visit

As a consolation prize, President Ford visited Spain on May 31-
June 1, 1975. [20] The reception given Ford was in much lower key
than that previously accorded Presidents Eisenhower and Nixon, and
he received considerable press criticism both in the United States and
in Europe. However, this is the price that major politicians sometimes have to pay to obtain their goals. The United States utilized the
president's visit to further its two-pronged policy toward Spain. On
the one hand, the United States was giving just enough attention to the
Spanish government to assure the continued presence of U.S. forces
in Spain, and on the other hand, it was quietly cultivating the key
Spaniards, including Juan Carlos, who would assume responsibility

when Franco was gone. In fact, President Ford was reported to have
spent more time with Prince Juan Carlos than with Franco himself.[21]

Eventually, on October 4, 1975, Secretary Kissinger and Foreign
Minister Cortina announced that "a new framework agreement govern-
ing cooperative relationships between the United States and Spain"
had been reached.[22] The agreement did not come easily, and it followed a dramatic occurrence in Madrid which effectively lowered
Spain's negotiating leverage, notwithstanding the obvious U.S. strategic interest in retaining the bases in light of other developments in
the south flank of Europe.

Outrage Against Spain

On September 26, 1975, General Franco refused to commute
the death sentences which had been imposed on five Basque ETA
terrorists for the alleged killed of Spanish police. The next day the
five men were executed by a firing squad.[23] This action caused a
flood of outrage and criticism of Spain, to the point that every country
in Western Europe recalled its ambassador from Madrid.[24] Secretary Kissinger seemed to take the position that some of the other
"many faces of America" should express the moral outrage that was
felt here, and simply stated that it was ". . . basically an internal
Spanish matter . . . ."[25] The secretary of state, however, did not
let the moment pass without exercising his new negotiating strength.
According to one reliable source, Kissinger told Cortina plainly that
there would have to be a moderation in the Spanish position on the
bases renewal if any kind of an agreement were to be reached with
the United States.[26] Thus, "the Framework Agreement" was reached
on October 4, 1975. Once again it was strictly an executive agreement without recourse to the Congress.[27]

Demise of Franco

On October 21, 1975, the Spanish government announced that
General Franco had suffered a heart attack. Two days later, on
October 23, the State Department announced that the new agreement
with Spain, contrary to an earlier pronouncement by Secretary
Kissinger and Foreign Minister Cortina, would be submitted to the
Congress for approval.[28] On October 30, 1975, General Franco was
so ill that he delegated his powers as head of state once again to
Juan Carlos. Finally on November 20, 1975, Franco died.

This event caused a two-month interregnum in the U.S. negotiations with Spain over the new treaty. Spain, of course, now had

momentum and leverage on its side. The new foreign minister, Areilza, called for "a gesture" or "real help" from the United States to the new monarchy.[29] On January 22, 1976, Ambassador McCloskey arrived in Madrid to undertake the final preparation with the Spanish negotiators for the signing which was to come. Secretary Kissinger arrived in Madrid on January 24, and after he met with the foreign minister and King Juan Carlos the new Treaty of Friendship and Cooperation was signed. Secretary Kissinger stated that he was confident Spain would progressively enter the framework "of all those human and political values that linked the Western World."[30] The Spanish foreign minister expressed Spanish satisfaction with the new agreement and termed it "a capital step in relations between the two countries."[31]

Clearly the United States had acted promptly to seize the constructive opportunity which had occurred with the passing of Franco. The leaders in Spain who had been involved in negotiations with the United States had also acted prudently. Whatever the force of the outside incidents which had affected the pace and the tone of the negotiations, and certainly there were some serious incidents, the resulting delay had been in the interest of both parties to the new agreement, which for the first time would be handled as a treaty and would be submitted to the Senate of the United States for approval.

Rather than attempt to analyze piece by piece the new treaty, the following is quoted from Secretary of State Kissinger's letter of submittal of the treaty to President Ford:

> The new agreement is in the form of a Treaty. This solemn form was deemed appropriate not only because of the wide scope and importance of the subject matter covered but also because both Spanish and United States authorities wanted to assure the soundest political basis for the new stage in United States–Spanish relations symbolized by the agreement.
>
> The treaty covers a broad spectrum of areas of mutual concern in United States–Spanish relations, with specific articles and supplementary agreements treating cooperation in the areas of economic affairs, education and culture, science and technology, and defense matters. It also provides an institutional framework to enhance the effectiveness of cooperation in all these areas. The principal new elements of substance are in this institutional area, and include the creation of a high-level United States–Spanish Council, to oversee the implementation of the entire agreement, and a set of subordinate bodies, including joint committees for the various areas of coop-

eration and a Combined Military Coordination and Planning Staff. The agreement specifies the military and non-military assistance to be given Spain over the five-year initial term of the agreement and grants to the United States essentially the same rights to use military facilities in Spain which it enjoyed under the 1970 arrangements. The principal changes in military facilities are a reduction and relocation of United States tanker aircraft within Spain and the establishment of a date for withdrawal of the nuclear submarine squadron from the Rota Naval Base.

Article I of the Treaty establishes the United States-Spanish Council, under the joint chairmanship of the Secretary of State of the United States and the Foreign Minister of Spain. The Council, which is to meet at least semi-annually, will have headquarters in Madrid, a permanent secretariat, and permanent representatives serving as deputies to the Chairmen. An important aspect of the new agreement is the integration of the military cooperation into the Council structure.

Article II calls for the development of closer economic ties between the United States and Spain. The agreement takes into account the current readiness of the Export-Import Bank to commit credits and guarantees of approximately $450 million to Spanish companies.

Article III provides for a broad program of scientific and technical cooperation. A total of $23 million would be provided by the United States in the form of grants to support this five-year program. One of the first matters of concern will be studies relating to a solar energy institute.

Article IV provides for a continuation and expansion of educational and cultural cooperation. The agreement contemplates a grant from the United States in the amount of $12 million to support this five-year program.

Articles V and VI of the Treaty deal with cooperation in the area of defense. The defense relationship which these provisions represent is woven firmly into the fabric of existing United States philosophy and planning for the defense of the North Atlantic area. It represents a decision to assist Spain in developing a role which will contribute actively to that defense, and provides transitional institutions to prepare the way for an appropriate Spanish role in NATO. These provisions do not constitute a security guarantee or commitment to defend Spain.

They do, however, constitute a recognition of Spain's importance as a part of the Western world.

To this end, a Combined Planning and Coordination Staff, with no command functions, is provided for by Supplementary Agreement Number Five, which sets forth a carefully drawn mandate and geographic area of common concern. All activities of the staff focus on the contingency of a general attack on the West. There is no commitment, express or implied, in the drawing up of the contingency plans.

To further the purposes of the Treaty, Spain grants the United States the right to use and maintain for military purposes those facilities in or connected with Spanish military installations which the United States has heretofore enjoyed, with the exception that the number of KC-135 tankers in Spain will be reduced to a maximum of five and the remaining tankers relocated; and that the nuclear submarines will be withdrawn from Spain by July 1, 1979, a date which corresponds with our changing requirements. In addition, the United States undertakes not to store nuclear devices or their components on Spanish soil.

The details of the military assistance to be provided Spain are that the United States would provide over the five year initial term of the Treaty, repayment guarantees under the Foreign Military Sales program for loans of $600 million, $75 million in defense articles on a grant basis, $10 million in military training on a grant basis, and a U.S. Air Force contribution on a cost-sharing basis, of up to $50 million for the aircraft control and warning network used by the U.S. Air Force in Spain. In addition, provision is made to transfer to Spain five naval vessels and 42 F4E aircraft.

The notes exchanged include United States assurances to Spain on settlement of damage claims which might result from nuclear incidents involving a United States nuclear powered warship reactor.

Associated with the Treaty and its supplementary agreements are an Agreement on Implementation and procedural annexes thereto which regulate such matters as the status of United States forces in Spain and the use of the facilities there. These documents are being provided to the Congress for its information.[32]

The Connection Enters a New Phase

The passing of Franco gave rise to questions regarding direction and conduct of Spanish foreign policy. After all, as Fernando Moran asserted, "The foreign policy of the Francoist era (1939-1975) is, in the final analysis, a policy defined, inspired or tempered by Franco himself."[33]

But the king and his advisors from the beginning left no doubt as to the route they would follow. They moved toward closer relations with the western and northern European democracies, all the while persevering in their claim to Gibraltar and in their tenuous hold in North Africa. At the same time, they continued to give priority to their relations with the United States.

Spaniards voiced general satisfaction with the 1976 treaty, which, after their previously unsuccessful efforts, had been upgraded in status. They could point out that the Americans still had to consult with them over any wartime use of the bases, and formal procedures were now required for such consultation through the new U.S.-Spanish Council. Spaniards could also point with satisfaction to the package of economic assistance which, by combining credits and loans, could be said to total more than $1 billion. (In the treaty hearings, the U.S. negotiators reported that the actual cost was only $34 million per year, or a total of $170 million.[34]) Finally, the Spanish press gave prominent attention to the planned withdrawal of the Polaris/Poseidon nuclear submarines from Rota, although this action, according to Pentagon reports, was in accord with the latest strategic plans of the United States.

In the United States, where press, members of Congress, and government officials had always taken considerable liberty in voicing their views on Spain's internal affairs, there was undisguised satisfaction over the new regime. Regarding the new treaty, Ambassador McCloskey observed that:

> the administration is firmly convinced that the treaty will
> benefit U.S. interests in Spain and Europe by giving posi-
> tive impetus to the transition now underway in Spain. We
> also believe that transition will facilitate the development
> of a more constructive and harmonious association be-
> tween Spain and the other West European countries. That
> is the broader objective of our policy. The United States
> supports Spain's progress toward democracy out of a
> dedication to human rights and out of the simple under-
> standing that we are all part of a wider Atlantic Commu-
> nity whose strength and cohesion demands that high
> standards in these matters be met and maintained by all

members. The treaty is a clear signal of our moral
support for Spain at this time.[35]

The Washington Post editorialized unabashedly:

Though Spain's progress is its own, the United States is
entitled to beam upon it with a patron's discreet favor.
The administration and the Congress, mutually supportive
if not always synchronized, have had a positive effect in
encouraging the forces of democracy. It was a wise move,
for instance, to convert the U.S.-Spanish bases agreement into a treaty—a step endowing the link with the extra
weight of Senate consent. Suitable executive-Congressional
formulations were worked out in and around the treaty to
express the Senate's hope that the treaty would advance
democracy, and to assure Spain of adequate continuity,
though not a blank check, in military support. The terms
of the treaty, by tightening the military and political links
between the two countries, furnished an additional measure of foreign assurance to Madrid as it tackled its deli-
cate domestic situation.[36]

As for the Congress, the Senate moved relatively fast to give
its advice and consent to the new treaty. The vote, taken on June 24,
1976, was 84-11. Yet, even with this strong evidence of support for
the treaty, the Senate showed its scars from the earlier bouts with
the executive branch over the connection with Spain by issuing four
significant "declarations" which could be interpreted as "strings"
attached to its ratification:

1. The treaty did not "create a mutual defense commitment."
2. Its action was in support of the eventual membership in NATO of
   "a democratic Spain."
3. It urged Spain to become a party to the Nuclear Non-Proliferation
   Treaty.
4. The Senate's approval was only for five years; if there were to be
   an extension, further action would be required.

THE SPANISH ECONOMY DISORDERED

The heady rush into political reform which took place in Spain
after Franco's disappearance from the scene, while gratifying to
democrats at home and abroad, did not facilitate removal of the
imbalances which barricaded every avenue to improved economic

performance. Rather, the efforts by the centrist governments which ruled Spain, 1975-1982, to satisfy too many politico-economic factions at once exacerbated inflation, eventually sent interest rates soaring, helped induce uninterrupted labor strife, undermined the confidence of savers and investors, and protracted the energy shortage. The seven years from 1975 to 1982 were to see both unemployment and inflation in Spain rise to levels not known in the country since the civil war.

Spain was not, of course, alone in experiencing economic trauma in this period. But the concern of Spanish politicians to survive in the elections and to hasten the restoration of political liberties, even at the expense of keeping the nation's economic house in order, made Spanish economic problems exceedingly severe. Unfortunately for the infant democracy, Franco's death in November 1975 immediately followed the sharpest and most widespread decline in economic activity in all the Western industrialized countries since the Second World War. OECD estimates of the rate of growth of the combined gross national (or domestic) products of the seven major OECD countries plunged from a positive 8.7 percent in the first half of 1973 to a negative 3.0 percent in the first half of 1975. While growth was partially restored in these countries in the latter part of 1975 and in subsequent years to 1980, the recovery came at the expense of enormous inflation in all of them.

Each of the oil importing countries faced complex and bewildering pressures on their economies at this time, and each had in place inadequate policy instruments—and indeed had inadequate understanding—for dealing with the problems. The increase in annual average petroleum prices from $1.90 per barrel (Saudi Arabia, Ras Tamura) in mid-1973 to $12.40 in 1977 had broad effects on both costs of production and levels of monetary demand in all the countries dependent on imports. Costs escalated unevenly across countries, depending on the degree of individual countries' dependence on imported supplies and on the ways in which petroleum costs were passed through to users. The cost increases also varied across industries within countries, depending on degrees of energy need in different lines of production and the degrees to which some users were favored over others in national policies. The spending in the oil importing countries that was diverted from other uses to petroleum reduced internal demand for domestic outputs and for non-oil imports, and the decline in real spending in these countries was not initially offset by increased spending by the oil exporting countries. Had governments done nothing to restore the buying power lost to oil exporting countries, output would have slowed in all those industries from which demand was being sapped until prices declined there by enough to restore the real purchasing power of money stocks. But prices, especially

wages, are sticky in modern societies, and unemployment could have
become politically intolerable before the requisite price adjustments
were completed. Partly because of this, most oil importing countries
dealt with the problem of flagging domestic production with policies
of demand expansion. Money supply growth, off somewhat to a 7.5
percent rate in industrialized countries in 1974, was restored to
double-digit levels in 1976 and 1978, and government operating deficits widened in many countries. The strategy that was widely and not
always consciously adopted, in short, was one of inflating all prices
to minimize the relative price and income distortion that the petroleum price rise would otherwise have caused.

The policy was at best only partially successful wherever it
was applied. While growth was temporarily restored to a degree in
countries like the OECD major seven (United States, Japan, Germany,
France, United Kingdom, Italy, and Canada) in 1976 and 1977, the
accompanying inflation introduced new price and wage distortions
which created new unemployment and dislocations; the inflation also
provided the OPEC countries opportunities for raising petroleum
prices again, opportunities which they vigorously exploited in 1978
and 1979 with another trebling of prices in dollar terms.

In this milieu, Spain's response to the external disturbance
was similar, except in degree, to that of other industrialized countries. While the momentum of its own real growth tendencies and the
monetary and price increases of 1973 and 1974 carried Spain into the
early months of the petroleum crisis period without the initial slowdown which hit other countries, inflation, flagging exports, and rising
import costs necessitated a clampdown on policies of demand expansion in mid-1975 which brought home the new economic situation.
Spanish unemployment nearly doubled, from only 2.6 percent of the
total labor force (including military forces) in 1974 to 5.0 percent
in 1976 and then rose to 5.6 percent in 1977. The significance of
these higher unemployment rates (OECD estimates) can be seen by
comparing them with the average rate of only 1.5 percent for the
1962-1967 period. Further, the 1976-1977 rates did not count the
numbers of people withdrawing in discouragement from the labor
force. The total labor force was shrinking after 1974 in spite of a
net return flow of workers from the rest of Europe as a result of the
disappearance of jobs there. Devaluation of the peseta by 10 percent
in February 1976, and by another 20 percent in June 1977, stemmed
a rapid loss of foreign exchange reserves but allowed the full measure
of internal inflation forces to be revealed.

The Arias Navarro and Suarez governments that followed
Franco's death, ruling through fragile parliamentary coalitions and
initially without the authority of a new constitution, only weakly con-
fronted the nation's economic ills. A pay policy and price freeze

quickly became untenable, and government budget deficits and monetary expansion fueled wage and price increases in 1976 and 1977 which gave Spain the dubious distinction in 1977, 1978, and 1979 of having the highest rate of inflation in Western Europe (excepting Iceland).

After the June 1977 elections gave some kind of a mandate to the government of Adolfo Suarez, his finance minister, Enrique Fuentes Quintana, attempted more vigorous tax collection, along with wage restraint softened by more generous unemployment programs. But Fuentes Quintana was forced to resign by reaction from the right in February 1978. The October 1977 "Pact of Moncloa" among all the leading political parties seemed momentarily to signal a compromise on income policies that could make an expansion of real output in the economy possible in conjunction with slowing inflation. The inflation already built in, however, by the devaluations of 1976 and 1977, by swelling government expenditures, and by the "second round" of oil price increases that began in 1978 doomed the pact to early insignificance.

In the late 1970s and early 1980s Spaniards have paid a price for their new freedoms. The progress of the economy in the 1960s was achieved in part by an opening of Spanish society to international interdependence. Whereas export demand constituted only 7.0 percent of total expenditures on Spanish products in 1959, it was 14.8 percent in 1979 and 18.1 percent in 1981. This greater dependence on foreign markets meant that Spain could not evade sharing in the protracted slowing of economic activity that took place in other industrialized countries after 1973, an impact the country might have avoided twenty years earlier. Similarly, Spanish growth had become dependent on an influx of foreign capital in the 1960s and early 1970s that slowed sharply in the context of Spanish political instability, trade union militancy, and escalating inflation in the later 1970s. Even emigration, Spain's escape valve of the 1960s, reversed itself, simultaneously flooding domestic labor markets, intensifying demands for unemployment benefits, enhancing labor militancy, and reducing the valuable stream of foreign exchange earnings remitted by Spaniards employed abroad. Trade unions, freed to organize, bargain collectively, and strike, fought for income gains in a society that could not provide such gains out of productivity growth; work stoppages and declining business profit margins then exacerbated the slowdown in economic progress.

DISMANTLING ECONOMIC CONTROLS

That Spain's adjustment to the global economic environment of the 1970s and 1980s was not more painful than it was may be credited in part to the meaures taken by the government to dismantle some of the economic controls that hung on after Franco as vestiges of his regime. The economy of the late 1970s and early 1980s needed all of the resiliency it could get, and the rigid employment laws, banking laws, and the investment laws favoring state industries were not, in 1975–1976, conducive to that flexibility. Liberalization—which was of course part and parcel of the restoration of political freedoms—was not, however, an unmitigated gain since, among other things, it partly opened the door to labor-management strife that had been suppressed for forty years.

Labor-Management Relations

The ability of laborers to influence their wages and working conditions by collective action increased somewhat even in the 1960s and was then codified in a revised Syndical Law of 1970 that allowed workers to elect their syndical officers and to assemble with these representatives in their plants. Still, legal and illegal strikes were rare until after Franco's death. In 1976 the number of reported work stoppages doubled, as compared to 1975, from 855 to 1,568, and the number of workers involved in the disputes increased seven fold (from 556 thousand to 3,639 thousand).[37] In 1976 and 1977 the government, in a series of laws, freed unions to organize and to engage freely in collective bargaining, greatly reducing the government's role in labor-management relations and providing new opportunities for employers to manage their employment levels. Workers were freed from compulsory participation in the old government-sponsored syndicates. A workers' statute and a basic law of employment, both of 1980, codified much of the assignment of rights and responsibilities among employers, unions, and the government and established the ground rules for collective bargaining.

Membership in freely organized unions grew rapidly after 1977 and at one point may have included 20 percent of the work force. By 1980, however, most unions were losing dues-paying members.[38] Unions everywhere are, of course, typically weak in times of high unemployment, so that the potentialities of trade unions in Spain have not yet been seriously tested.

The identification of various unions with particular political parties tends to make of the unions instruments for political threat as well as instruments for bargaining on wages and working conditions. This marriage of political and economic power, which is in the European tradition of unionism but not the American, has created, of course, some challenges to stability for democratic processes in Spain. A movement within the small independent unions to coalesce into an apolitical "third force" in the labor markets had by 1982 made little progress.

The Communist-dominated Workers' Commissions (CCOO) lost, by the beginning of the 1980s, their early plurality of total union membership so that they ranked more evenly with the Socialist Union General de Trabajadores (UGT). The other significant union with national strength was the Christian Union Sindical Obrera (USO), but the USO was, in 1980, still not large enough to merit a seat at the national wage bargaining table.[39] The dominant labor bargaining agent in the industrialized Basque region was the Basque Regional Union (STV). Numerous small "independent" unions represented some or all workers in individual plants and areas.

The collective bargaining process emerging in 1981-1982 was one carried out on several levels. In January 1980, even before the final passage into law of the Workers' Statute, the Spanish Employers Association (CEOE) and the Socialist UGT signed a two-year Framework Bargaining Agreement (Acuerdo Marco Interconfederal, or AMI) which set the outline for working condition settlements on a national basis. Actual contracts were hammered out at regional, sectoral, or plant levels, the level of negotiation being a matter for union and management agreement. While the Communist-oriented CCOO rejected the AMI as a basis for 1980 settlements, USO and the Association of Small and Medium Employers (CEPYME) accepted it, and "An analysis of final contracts in 1980, signed at the level where they governed the wages and working conditions of the employee, indicated that 62.3 percent of all contracts fell within the AMI pattern."[40] The AMI called for 1980 wage settlements to fall within a range of 13 to 16 percent increases (firms in special distress could settle below this level) with modifications upward if consumer prices should be rising at more than a 13.5 percent rate during the first six months of the year. The agreement also called for a 6.3 percent reduction in the average number of hours worked per year—spreading the work among employees by minimizing use of overtime—and for reducing the retirement age to 64. It addressed issues of productivity, absenteeism, dealing with disputes, and union rights.

The national agreement for 1982, known as the ANE and signed in June 1981, called for limitations on wage increases to a 9-11 percent range, with consumer prices expected to rise by 15 percent. By October 1981, however, that agreement was unraveling because of employer association objections to government plans for new business taxes and a government offer to compensate unions for properties seized during the civil war—a proposal the CEOE saw as a payoff to the leftist political parties.

Wage increases steadily outpaced consumer price increases in Spain after 1975 and hence, with productivity growth stagnant, were a contributing factor in the inflation and in the exacerbation of unemployment. As of August 1982 the official index of wages, based on 1975, had reached a level 43 percent above the similarly based index of consumer prices. Unemployment had at that time also reached 16 percent.

Financial Reforms

Dismantling of controls over financial markets has not proceeded with the same speed as institutional change in Spanish labor-management relations, but important liberalizing changes have occurred.

Perhaps most significant has been the 1978 decree permitting foreign banks to operate in Spain. Prior to the decree, only four foreign banks—two French (Credit Lyonnais and Societe Generale), one British (Bank of London and South America), and one Italian (Banca Nazionale del Lavoro)—had Spanish offices, and all of these operations predated the civil war. By 1981, twenty-three foreign banks were operating in Spain.[41] The newcomers are generally limited to the wholesale money markets, being permitted no more than three branches. In February 1981, however, Barclay's Bank of London was allowed to buy the weakened Banco de Valladolid which has branches in all major Spanish cities, introducing a foreign bank to the retail market. Naturally apprehensive of the competition from foreigners, the Spanish banking community blocked New York's Citibank from purchasing a part of Spain's second largest finance house early in 1981.

The Big Seven Spanish banks[42] continue to dominate commercial banking.

> The so-called Big Seven account for 46 percent of total
> capital reserves, 52 percent of commercial lending and
> 58 percent of deposits. If their affiliates were included,
> these figures would all be 10 percent higher. With 76
> commercial banks, 26 industrial (investment) banks, and
> 23 foreign banks now operating in Spain, the dominance
> of the Big Seven is remarkable.[43]

Banco Urquijo is perhaps Spain's leading traditional investment bank, and the Rumasa group of firms (including 18 banks), formerly controlled by Jose Maria Ruiz-Mateos, was a new and aggressive financial group before its nationalization in February 1983.

The cajas de ahorro, regional savings banks, held one-third of Spain's private financial resources in 1981 and function more and more like commercial banks.

Deregulation has resulted from efforts of the Bank of Spain to gain control over money supply growth, from desires by government authorities to improve the efficiency with which Spanish markets allocate capital, and from the difficulties banks have encountered in the milieu of economic stagnation in the 1970s. In an excellent survey of "Monetary Control by Control of the Monetary Base: The Spanish Experience," Pedro Martínez Méndez[45] has noted that:

> until the early 1970s a monetary policy designed to guide developments in monetary aggregates or interest rates on a continuous basis did not exist. Instead, very restrictive action relying heavily on quantitative control of bank credit was taken intermittently on an ad hoc basis at time of crisis. Despite its effectiveness in the short run this usually had very disruptive effects on economic activity.
>
> After a final such episode of monetary restraint in 1969 the authorities decided that the time had come for a more gradualist and continuous approach to monetary policy. From then onwards there was no real alternative to defining monetary objectives in terms of growth of the money stock and to controlling monetary expansion by controlling the monetary base.[46]

The Bank of Spain could not use market interest rates as a target for monetary policy because there was in Spain in the 1970s no free market for funds that would exhibit interest rates that were meaningful indicators of changing credit scarcity. Throughout the Franco period artificially low legal interest rate ceilings insured that the demand for bank credit exceeded the supply so that credit was normally rationed by the banks. The banks were obliged, on the other hand, to buy low-yielding public and private sector bonds and otherwise to grant credit to particular industries.[47] Some public and private borrowers even had unconditional access to the Bank of Spain before 1971[48] so that the bank was without power to limit the expansion of its own credit. Banks held few bonds that were negotiable, and the Treasury offered no short-term securities for public sale. Exchange controls inhibited free movement of funds into and out of Spain. Martínez Méndez notes that "a side effect of these regulations was that holdings of fixed-interest securities by non-banks became very small," and that as a consequence secondary securities markets "almost vanished."[49]

Some, but by no means all, of these limitations on the growth of effective money and capital markets were removed during the 1970s. Government authorization of securities that gave the issuer automatic access to central bank credit ended in 1971; interest rates on bank loans and deposits with maturities greater than two years were freed in 1974; and ceilings on similar rates for maturities of more than one year were lifted in 1977.[50] Interest ceilings were still in effect on loans and deposits of less than one year in 1981, but banks frequently accepted one year deposits at above ceiling rates and imposed no penalty for early withdrawal. Starting in 1977 a gradual reduction was begun in the share of deposits that banks and cajas de ahorro were required to place in public investments or the central bank. Ratios that were as high as 80 percent for the cajas in 1977 were only 60 percent in 1981, and reductions continued into 1982; interest earnings on the mandated loans, meanwhile, were made more generous.

Bank failures, almost unknown in Spain until 1978, became common after that as a result of the hardships encountered by the banks' customers. Twenty banks failed or required assistance between 1978 and November 1982, the largest of which was the Banca Catalona Group, of Barcelona, Spain's twelfth largest. The Corporación Bancaria (popularly known as "the bank hospital"), with 50 percent funding from the Bank of Spain, and the Fondo de Guarantía de Depositos, the Bank of Spain's agency for deposit insurance, have been involved in all of the bank rescue efforts.

Foreign banks have introduced a market for acceptances to Spain, floating interest rates, and bank syndication of peseta denominated loans. They have participated in a new and active interbank market.

Spanish officials were, in 1980 and 1981, seeking to revive Spain's four stock exchanges which provided about 30 percent of business external financing in 1970 but only 10 percent in 1980.[51]

Liberalizing measures have probably increased the efficiency with which Spanish real savings are converted into real capital in recent years, but obstacles remain. Martínez Méndez mentions several steps which would improve the flexibility of bank portfolios and hence the responsiveness of the money market to change: the full liberalization of interest rates; the issue of Treasury bills by regular auction; the abolition of remaining bank compulsory investment ratios; and the freeing of exchange controls to permit banks to engage in foreign currency swaps. He goes on to say that "Progress will be slow, as traditional views and entrenched economic interests have to be overcome. But there is powerful logic in the envisaged changes, and this will make it very difficult to postpone them indefinitely."[52]

Industrial Policy

Shifts in government policies toward the industrial sector of the economy have been stimulated by the necessity of containing the rampant inflation, a desire to strengthen and indeed salvage some well developed but depressed industries, and a desire by politically centrist governments to reduce government regulation and ownership.

Spanish policy toward energy, for example, in the years following the crisis of 1973-1974, initially protected energy users, especially industrial users, from the full force of the price rises. Petroleum imports constituted nearly 70 percent of Spain's total energy use in 1974, and the first round of price increases raised the petroleum import bill from $840 million in 1972 to $3.5 billion annually in 1974-1975. A state marketing monopoly, through its trading losses, provided subsidies to the products of Spain's refineries—gasoline and especially heating and diesel oil for industrial uses.

A ten-year national energy plan adopted in 1979 changed this energy policy and introduced steps increasingly to require all users of petroleum products to pay such products' full costs. Between January 1980 and the spring of 1981 energy prices were adjusted upward three times so that gasoline prices rose 33 percent, diesel fuel 77 percent, fuel oil 90 percent, and electricity 67 percent.[53] The energy plan has anticipated the extensive substitution of coal for petroleum, especially in electricity generation, and the addition of nuclear generating capacity. A public trading corporation, CARBOEX, was created to insure the availability of imported coal as that fuel becomes necessary.[54]

In other areas, the government has moved to aid in restructuring sectors of the economy threatened by protracted economic depression. Legal arrangements for aid to the producers of specialized steel were set out in the royal decree of October 3, 1980, and provided for a joint stock company to be set up with participation by the national and Basque region governments. The company was charged with adjusting industry supply to demand, raising productivity, improving marketing of products, strengthening company financial positions, and facilitating mergers. A similar policy has been followed with a sector of the home appliance industry and with the basic integrated steel industry; further plans have been made for reorganizing the textile industry. INI guaranteed a $400 million loan to the steel industry in late 1981 that was syndicated by eight Spanish banks.[55] Reflecting the intense international competition in steel products, the U.S. International Trade Commission, in December 1982, approved countervailing duties on $4.8 million of stainless steel wire rods from Spain on grounds that the production of the rods benefited from Spanish subsidies. Spain's steel industry, meanwhile, was a major user of U.S. iron and steel scrap and coal.

INI, the Instituto Nacional de Industria, came under increasing attack by leaders of the private sector after 1975 because of the preferential treatment it received from the state. Some unprofitable INI enterprises have been offered for sale—most notably SEAT, Spain's state-owned automobile assembly operation. FIAT, of Italy, which provided designs, technology, and components to SEAT from its start, has declined to take over the firm, and a search has therefore had to continue for a foreign buyer. The possibility of a Japanese purchaser of SEAT interacts with Spain's negotiations for entry to the European Economic Community since some Common Market countries, especially France, oppose acquisition by the Japanese of another production base inside the customs union area.[56]

NOTES

1. New York Times, November 26, 1973.
2. Washington Star News, November 2, 1973.
3. Washington Post, December 20, 1973.
4. Ibid.
5. Ibid., December 21, 1973.
6. Time, December 31, 1973.
7. Washington Post, February 13, 1974.
8. ABC (Madrid), July 10, 1974.
9. Ibid.
10. Ibid.
11. Washington Post, June 15, 1974.
12. Spanish Base Treaty Hearings, p. 23.
13. Informaciones (Madrid), November 6, 1974.
14. Ya (Madrid), November 6, 1974.
15. ABC (Madrid), November 7, 1974.
16. Ibid.
17. Christian Science Monitor, June 26, 1970.
18. Ya (Madrid), November 7, 1974.
19. Ibid.
20. Washington Post, May 7, 1975.
21. Ibid., June 2, 1975.
22. International Herald Tribune (Paris), October 6, 1975.
23. Ibid., September 29, 1975.
24. Ibid.
25. Washington Post, September 30, 1975.
26. Chamorro and Fontes, Las Bases Norte Americanas en España, p. 292.
27. International Herald Tribune (Paris), October 6, 1975.
28. Ibid.
29. Ibid., December 18, 1975.
30. Chamorro and Fontes, Las Bases Norte Americanas en España, p. 303.

31. International Herald Tribune (Paris), January 26, 1976.

32. Hearings, Treaty of Friendship and Cooperation with Spain, pp. 77-79.

33. Armero, prologue written by Fernando Moran (presently foreign minister in the Socialist government), p. 13.

34. Spanish Base Treaty Hearings, p. 44.

35. Ibid., p. 9.

36. Washington Post, November 24, 1976.

37. Data from the Syndical Organization, cited in Eric N. Baklanoff, The Economic Transformation of Spain and Portugal (New York: Praeger, 1978), p. 92.

38. U.S. Embassy, Madrid, "Labor Report for Spain, 1978 through 1980," June 1, 1981 (mimeographed), p. 2.

39. The Workers' Statute requires that unions represent 10 percent of elected worker delegates to plant bargaining committees in order to sit on regional, sector, or national bargaining councils.

40. U.S. Embassy, Madrid, "Labor Report for Spain, 1978 through 1980," p. 25.

41. "The Old Guard Backs into the Future," World Business Weekly, April 13, 1981, p. 29.

42. Banco Español de Credito, Banco Central, Banco Hispano Americano, Banco de Bilbao, Banco de Santander, Banco de Vizcaya, and Banco Popular Español, ranked in order of size of total deposits.

43. World Business Weekly, April 13, 1981, p. 31.

44. Rumasa (from Ruiz-Mateos, S.A.) in 1982 added Gallerias Preciados, one of Spain's two largest retailing chains, to its portfolio, and then Sears' operations in Spain. When, in February 1983, government bank investigators declared Rumasa's banks to be unsound, the entire conglomerate was nationalized.

45. Bank for International Settlements, The Monetary Base Approach to Monetary Control (Basle, September 1980), reprinted as Documento de Trabajo Nr 8005 by Servicio de Estudios del Banco de España.

46. Ibid., p. 2.

47. These requirements constituted what were called the "privileged circuits" for funds.

48. Most notably the state railways and certain entities of INI.

49. Bank for International Settlements, The Monetary Base Approach to Monetary Control, p. 1.

50. Ibid., p. 23, note 2.

51. World Business Survey, April 13, 1981, p. 35.

52. Bank for International Settlements, The Monetary Base Approach to Monetary Control, p. 22.

53. Spain, OECD Annual Surveys, May 1981 (Paris: Organisation for Economic Cooperation and Development), p. 28.

54. Ibid., p. 28.
55. Wall Street Journal, October 9, 1981.
56. See Business Week, October 12, 1981, p. 63.

The United States and Spain—
Present and Future

SPAIN REBORN

Spain has always been a portrait too big for its frame. Its own writers and historians have resorted to hyperbole to describe what Spain is, what it isn't, and what it seeks to be. Thus, it should be no surprise that outside observers have done the same thing, floundering from one exaggeration to another in trying to describe Spain. There is certainly part truth to all that has been said. Yet truth is always elusive.

Since Franco's death, Spain has settled down to its task of national reorientation. Outsiders may laud or criticize, but Spaniards seem no longer to mind. Their timetable is no longer Franco's, nor that of any external influence, including American; instead, it responds to their own demands. They can now follow Robert Frost's advice: "Take what is given and make it over your way."

Spain has, in effect, been "born again" not once but twice. The first rebirth was primarily social and economic, as Spain marshaled its impressive human resources to rebuild the country, taking advantage of the material resources provided under the agreements. The second rebirth was moral and political, coming in logical sequence after Franco's death. The people of Spain had been stigmatized by the Franco government for three and one-half decades. They had also felt the ostracism of an international community which condemned Franco. One Spanish writer, self-exiled during Franco's regime, even thought that the Spanish people were "necessarily sick," and that their "convalescence [after Franco] may last as long as the illness did."[1] He was wrong, as we now know. Rubottom's friend of three decades ago was right when he said "we shall outlast Franco."

THE POLITICAL MIRACLE

The "reborn" Spain turned almost overnight to more democratic political institutions. With incredible speed, the new government, headed by King Juan Carlos, erased the Franco image and established new democratic processes. No sooner were such processes established, however, than they began to be tested. Both in the emergence of conflicts and in the process of conflict resolution it was almost as if Spaniards had been secretly rehearsing their parts for democracy through the many years that the process had been suppressed. Whatever their motivation and incentives, the Spanish people since 1975 have accomplished a political miracle to match the startling economic achievements of the 1960s.

The first year after Franco, 1976, was one of survival, testing, and transition. During the first six months, the King maintained most of the Franco cabinet, including the prime minister, Carlos Arias Navarro. Fortunately, the cabinet included Foreign Minister José María de Areilza, who had a liberalizing influence on his colleagues, and who was experienced in dealing with the United States.

The new government early lifted the ban on political parties, except the Communists, Anarchists, and Separatists. Next came freedom of the press, marked by the founding of the liberal paper El Pais, "which soon came to resemble a Spanish mixture of the Washington Post, New York Times and Le Monde."[2] Notwithstanding these moves, it was soon obvious that the extremes to the left, notably the labor leaders and the Separatists, were going to test the new government as much as were the forces on the right, led by the military who preferred the Franco method.

The king moved unerringly toward a democratic regime, "fearing that there was greater danger from immobility and caution than from fundamental change."[3] The king received public support from Adolfo Suarez Gonzalez, the secretary general of the Movement, a body of former Falangists, JONS (labor syndicates), Traditionalists, and others who had come together under Franco's pressure. When he was appointed to one of the civil governorships, Suarez stated that "the immense majority of the Spanish people want a just and peaceful democracy, and they will have it."[4] Later, in the Cortes, the newly important Spanish parliament, he argued that the government should encourage democracy by accepting the fact that Spain is a pluralistic society.

HIGH AMERICAN EXPECTATIONS

The United States continued to play a significant part in Spain's testing time. Its expectation that Spain would move toward democracy was clearly manifested even before Franco's death. In fact, from the time of the late 1940s, Congress, press, and church commentaries had emphasized that the American connection with the Franco government was a matter of security and expediency, not an alliance.

In June 1976 King Juan Carlos and the queen visited the United States. According to all reports, their visit was an outstanding success, both in their personal capacities and in their representative capacity on behalf of a nation in rapid transition from authoritarian to popular rule.

SUAREZ HEADS REFORM GOVERNMENT

Shortly after returning from the United States, in July 1976, King Juan Carlos reorganized his government. He chose Adolfo Suarez as prime minister who, the previous month, had defended the legalization of political parties by an all-embracing statement designed to attract support from every sector in the political spectrum. Suarez had argued that it was possible for Spain to have "a Democratic Socialism infused with a strong nationalist sentiment and a modern conservatism, integrated with the European perspective."[5] Suarez's uncompromising public support of the king got him the premiership, but nobody was sure that he could deliver on his program of national unification. In his pro-reform cabinet, he included Marcelino Oreja Aguirre, as foreign minister. The latter had been closely identified with efforts to integrate Spain into the Common Market as well as NATO, believing that both would contribute to the democratization of Spain.

The king's second government moved rapidly on a number of political and social reforms. It granted a limited amnesty to all persons sent to prison for ideological-political crimes; it announced the form and timing of elections (for the spring or early summer of 1977); it established contacts with the opposition for purposes of reassurance; and it informed the Church it was willing to drop its participation in the appointment of bishops under the Madrid-Vatican Concordat of 1953.[6]

Soon it became apparent that Suarez's intention was to form a government built around the Christian Democratic Party, encompassing both the left and the right sectors. His hope was to build a protective wall against the extreme right Francoist wing as well as against the Communist and Socialist left wing. While in the end that strategy failed, Suarez's reforms left an indelible impression.

The king continued to assert himself. His next move assured the success of his democratizing efforts. When the top army commander, Lt. General Fernando de Santiago, refused to carry out the reforms and even wrote to his fellow officers to express his concern, the king moved promptly to fire him. After some sparring, Santiago was replaced by Lt. General Gutierrez Mellado, who had been passed over by Franco. He first set about reshaping the army to make it more compatible to the forces of the NATO countries. Then he reorganized its personnel in such a way as to remove a large number, estimated at 3,000, of right wing officers from the active duty list. Finally, with the support of the air force, the military reform program, designed to remove the military from politics, was approved.

The close of 1976 saw the democratization of the Cortes. Under the Francoist system, the Cortes had "organic" representation, under which positions were held by heads of families, the military, labor, professional organizations, and the like, all in a representative capacity. The new plan, calling for popular representation through legalized political parties, was submitted to a national referendum and was approved by nearly 95 percent of those voting.

FULL SPEED AHEAD WITH REFORM

In 1977 the tempo of reform quickened In rapid succession, strikes were authorized, trade unions were legalized, and full amnesty was granted to all political prisoners.

On June 15, 1977, the first free elections in forty years were held in Spain. Suarez's center coalition group, UDC, got 165 of 350 seats in the Cortes, or 35 percent; the Socialists, led by Felipe Gonzalez, garnered 118 seats, or 26 percent of the vote; and the Communists managed to get only 20 seats, or 7.5 percent of the vote.

This period was not without trauma. Two months before the election, the Suarez cabinet announced a royal decree dissolving the 30-year-old National Movement, the very heart of the political system under Franco. Two weeks later, the government lifted the ban on the Communist Party. The latter action, in particular, raised the hackles of some of the military officers, but their protest had already been neutralized by the appointment of new reform-minded commanding officers. There were civilian objections, too. The former interior minister, Manuel Fraga Iribarne, soon to become the head of the right wing Popular Alliance coalition, called the legalization of the Communist Party "a veritable coup d'etat, a grave political mistake and a legal farce."

The signal was "full speed ahead." The Suarez government, backed by a resolute king, must have decided that the Spanish people, stimulated by their heady new political freedom, could go all the way in the liberalization process. Whatever warning signals were shown, they were not considered to be serious threats to the regime. In July 1977, a family planning seminar was announced, shattering another taboo within Spain. Thirty-one experts from all over the country participated in a week-long seminar devoted to the subject.

On September 29, 1977, the "Generalitat" was restored to Catalonia. Since the fourteenth century that body had been the symbol of self-government of that province. In accepting its restoration, the signatories in Catalonia promised that they would respect the unity of Spain.

The moves by the Spanish government captured international attention, and the government capitalized on its new acclaim. On November 24, 1977, Spain joined the Council of Europe. At the same time, Foreign Minister Oreja signed the European Convention on Human Rights and also the Convention on Legal Rights of Migrant Workers.

By now, Spaniards and outsiders alike knew that Franco was truly dead. As for his ghost, Francoism, it had no effective leadership, and had lost its way. To be sure, small factions of "true believers" were still present, notably among the uniformed services, but they were kept off-balance by the government's daring initiatives. (When they struck on February 23, 1981, it was too late.) There was a much larger number of "doubters" who yearned more for the old "order" than the new "freedom," but their passive concern never became activist, and gradually they were co-opted by the successes of Spain's new democracy.

In the spring of 1978, Spaniards witnessed an event that had major domestic and external implications. On April 30, the Socialist Workers Party (PSOE) and the Popular Socialist Party (PSP) merged into one political grouping. This was a historic occasion since the Socialist Party in Spain, founded in 1897, had always been divided, one faction favoring the democratic, pluralistic, and moderate approach, and one favoring a revolutionary approach to politics. The young leader of the PSOE, Felipe Gonzalez, pulled off this coup. This meant that the Socialists controlled 124 votes in the 350-seat Cortes.

The event turned into a foreign relations extravaganza. The formal ceremonies attendant to the merger were attended by Mitterand, Socialist leader of France, Soares, Socialist leader of Portugal, and Craxi, Socialist leader of Italy.

Meanwhile, the Suarez government was slowly giving ground to strident demands for "autonomy" by the Spanish provinces. The first concessions were made to the Basques in the northern provinces of Viscaya, Guipúzcoa, and Alva; concessions also were made to Catalonia, on the Mediterranean coast. However, on March 19, 1978, limited autonomy was also granted to Galicia, Valencia, Aragon, and

the Canary Islands. Then Catalonia proved not to be satisfied with its
degree of political autonomy. It asked for, and got on June 23, 1978,
official approval to offer the Catalan language as a required course
in the schools of the provinces.

Only time will tell whether the Madrid government's concessions
to the demands of those provinces wanting autonomy will lead to a
stronger federated Spain, or to the nation's breakup. Madrid has
taken a calculated gamble that such gestures will so strengthen the
moderates within the autonomy movement that they can suppress
terrorism and extremism in their ranks.

NEW CONSTITUTION

The Cortes approved a new constitution in draft in late October
1978. On December 6 the Spanish voters overwhelmingly approved
the constitution by a majority of 88 percent, and on December 27,
1978, it became effective. With the new constitution in place, the
Cortes two days later, December 29, dissolved itself and called for
new elections on March of the following year.

The constitution was divided into ten parts: (1) general principles;
(2) fundamental rights and duties; (3) the crown; (4) the parliament;
(5) the government; (6) the judiciary; (7) economy and housing; (8) the
autonomous territories; (9) the constitutional tribune; and (10) constitutional reform. The constitution tended to favor traditional civil
rights; it provided a system of regulations for regional autonomy;
and it stripped the chief of state (the king) of much of his powers and
placed them in the parliament.

Even so, there was considerable criticism from the left against
the powers retained by the chief of state and the head of government.
The left also objected to the appointment powers left in the hands of
the executive, to the reserve powers clause, and to the limitations
placed on motions of censure directed against the head of government.[7] The constitution provided for the members of the Senate to
be elected on the basis of territorial representation: the provinces
have four senators each, the large islands three, the small islands
one, the African cities of Ceuta and Melilla one each, and the autonomous communities each designate one senator plus others at the
rate of one per million population. The Senate retained its 208 seats,
but the king's appointed senators (41) were abolished.[8]

In the spring elections, Suarez was overwhelmingly returned
to the premiership. The center coalition UCD got 167 seats, nine
short of a majority of the 350 seats, but it won 119 of the 208 seats
in the Senate. Suarez was reelected premier in the Cortes by a vote
of 183 to 141.

Ten days later the first local elections were held since the death of Franco. The UCD won 31 percent of these votes, the Socialists won 29 percent, and the Communists obtained 13 percent. As an indicator of its declining approval and of things to come, the UCD won in only one industrial city, Oviedo.

The debate in the Socialist Party during this time attracted public attention. Felipe Gonzalez, party head, wanted to retain those partisans who were essentially Marxist in their outlook, but he ruled out any Communists who favored "democratic centralism."[9] He was determined that, if Communists came under the Socialist tent, they would have to be "just as democratic" within the party as they professed to be outside. He obviously had learned the lessons of history well. It is known that the Socialist Party came to regret its ties with the Communists during the Spanish Civil War. Gonzalez's principal effort after he became party leader was to consolidate democracy in the party.

"NEW" SPAIN'S EXTENSIVE OUTREACH

The presence of "new" Spain began to be felt throughout the world. In mid-1978, the king and queen visited mainland China. In early 1979, Foreign Minister Oreja visited Moscow, and later that year Spain was paid a return visit by Soviet Foreign Minister Gromyko. The head of the Palestine Liberation Organization (PLO), Yassir Arafat, likewise dropped in to pay his respects to the new government.

Traditionally Spain has always accorded high priority to its relations with the Vatican. Whether one sees the church in Spain as an obstacle to progress, or as the activist leader of social reform, no one questions the importance of the church role there. Arnold Hottinger has described the Spanish church as experiencing "a profound crisis" in the 1970s. He declared that Spain is undergoing a process of "dechristianization." In order to regain credibility with an increasingly knowledgeable membership, the Spanish Bishops' Conference has quietly assumed a more progressive stance.[10]

Consolidated and strengthened by, first, popular elections, and, second, approval of a new constitution, the Spanish government on January 3, 1979, signed a new Concordat with the Vatican. Both parties welcomed the change, Madrid in order to reassert control over education and other aspects of national life, the Vatican in order to regain authority heretofore divided over clerical appointments in Spain. The negotiations lasted two and a half years. It is interesting that the government could make an agreement with the Vatican while Spanish Catholics are deeply divided about their religion and the Spanish church is deeply divided about itself.[11]

Interesting, too, is the fact that Spanish priests are the center thrust of the Catholic Church in Latin America, even though their strength at home is eroding.

In the conduct of its foreign relations, Spain has become more and more eclectic. It trades with the world, it receives tourists from all over the world, and it must make the narrow distinctions that are required of a major nation in this complex world. There are few if any certainties on which it can count, and marginal advantages from any decision must be offset against marginal costs. So, like all nations, Spain had to assign priorities, and, from 1975, Spanish governments had set no foreign policy priority higher than admission to NATO and the Common Market. With Franco out of the picture, the most formidable obstacle to achievement of these goals had been removed. While some dissenting voices to NATO membership were heard inside Spain, even among the military, these voices were not influential enough to stop the steady push toward a NATO application. Partly because of Spain's long-time American connection, NATO was a more readily attainable goal than the Common Market.

One of the most knowledgeable Spaniards on subjects pertaining to security is the journalist Antonio Sanchez-Gijon. In his book Spain and NATO, he gives five reasons for joining NATO:

1. It is not entirely legitimate for Spain to accept the advantages of EEC (Common Market) membership without sharing the responsibilities of NATO, which, in a sense, is the political (and security) projection of the EEC.
2. The bilateral agreement with the United States does not provide as much security as would the multilateral arrangement with NATO.
3. Membership in NATO would promote military-technological transfers and lead to greater military specialization and professionalism.
4. Membership could speed the return of Gibraltar to Spain in part because it would increase Spain's political leverage and in part because Spain would carry a greater responsibility for NATO's defenses in the South Atlantic.
5. If Spain chose neutrality, Moscow would certainly try to neutralize Spain permanently. [12]

Many Spaniards disagreed with Sanchez-Gijon's thesis. In 1980, Fernando Moran, subsequently foreign minister in the Socialist government, wrote that, by becoming involved in NATO, Spain "would automatically incur serious risks for millions of its citizens."[13] He admitted there was also risk in the bilateral agreements with the United States, but said this was less than the risk Spain would incur by joining NATO. One of the Socialist party campaign planks was that parliamentary approval was not enough to authorize Spain's entry to NATO. The Socialists demanded a national referendum on the subject.

Nevertheless, Spain formally applied for NATO membership on June 15, 1981. After a year's wait, Spain received the required unanimous vote and became the sixteenth member of the alliance. Its official acceptance was deposited on May 30, 1982.

At the start of the Iranian crisis, In January 1980, Prime Minister Suarez visited Washington. While there he expressed public support for the United States during that ordeal. In June, President Carter became the first American president of Democratic persuasion to visit Spain. It was obvious that the U.S.-Spanish connection was still important to both nations.

In April 1980 Spain became the thirty-fourth member of the Economic Commission for Latin America (ECLA). This gave Spain a permanent seat at the ECLA headquarters in Santiago, Chile, and was evidence of its continuing interest in stronger economic ties, alongside its traditional political and cultural ties, with that region.

Foreign Minister Oreja, on April 10, 1980, signed an agreement "in principle" with the British foreign minister, Lord Carrington, to reopen the land frontier between Gibraltar and Spain. Equally important, they agreed that the two nations would enter into negotiations on the status of Gibraltar "in accord with United Nations' resolutions." In fact, the closing of the frontier at La Linea-Gibraltar had hurt Spain more than it had hurt Great Britain. After a decade's experience with the border closed, the consensus among Spaniards appeared to be that, now that Spain had joined NATO, let the issue of Gibraltar cool, wait for time to prove their claim, and meanwhile, take economic advantage of the nation's proximity to Gibraltar.

THE FIRST SEVERE CHALLENGE

In the face of rising inflation and growing unemployment, Prime Minister Suarez resigned his position on January 29, 1981. Timing his move to take advantage of the government crisis, Lt. Colonel Antonio Tejero Molina on February 23 led a small but determined band of Francoist diehards in an attempted military coup to overthrow the elected government. Molina himself was an officer in the Civil Guard. He, under armed threat, actually took control of the Cortes for several hours. The enthralling action was seen live on TV in Spain and later was rebroadcast throughout the world. The coup attempt failed, thanks to the courage of the king and to the fact that the Spanish people stood firm in their commitment to democratic government, in spite of the uncertainty and political chaos that reigned for several hours.

On June 3, 1982, sixteen months after the attempted coup, the two leaders, including Lt. General Jaime Milans de Bosch, once a military adviser to the king, were sentenced to thirty years in prison. Many observers thought that the delicacy with which the government handled the insurrectionists represented excessive compromise with the political right wing. Nevertheless, in this way ended the most severe challenge yet to the Spanish people's latest attempt at self rule.

Two days after the attempted coup, February 25, 1981, Leopoldo Calvo Sotelo, the new leader of the UDC coalition was sworn in as prime minister of the Spanish government. His father before him had been prime minister during the 1930s. The new foreign minister, Perez Llorca, was a strong backer of Spain's entry into NATO.

Later that year, on October 20, the right wing Popular Alliance (AP) led by Fraga won more than a third of the seats in the Galician regional parliamentary elections, beating the UDC, which got only 24 seats, and the Socialists, who got 17 seats. Because of the attempted coup earlier in the year, considerable political significance was given to this victory by the right wing group in Galicia. However, in the light of subsequent political developments within Spain, it appears that the vote was more a mere expression of Galician conservatism than a reflection of a national trend.

In fact, just seven months later, May 24, 1982, in the Andalusian regional election, the Socialists won 52 percent of the popular vote and gained 66 out of 109 seats in the provincial parliament. This was in fact an augury of what was to come. Calvo Sotelo's position deteriorated all through 1982 until he resigned and called for elections, which were held on October 29. The Socialists won 201 (46 percent) of the 350 seats, followed by the rightist Alianza Popular, AP, which got 106 (25.3 percent) of the seats. The centrist group which had governed Spain until that time, the UDC, gained only 12 seats in the parliament. In the Senate the Socialists won 134 out of 208 seats. The Communists did so poorly, winning only five seats in the Cortes out of 350, that their long-time leader, Santiago Carrillo, resigned as head of the party a few days after the election. On December 2, Socialist Felipe Gonzalez, age 40, was sworn in as prime minister of the Spanish government.

BASE AGREEMENTS—TIME FOR RENEWAL

While the U.S.-Spanish Connection still had significance for both parties, it was obvious in 1981 that the connection no longer commanded the priority attention that it had received in its earlier years. Even though the 1976 treaty was due to expire in September, the negotiations seemed to proceed at an unhurried pace. Each meeting of the principal negotiators was covered in the Madrid press, and sometimes in the American press, but the stories carried no tone of urgency.

Spaniards were preoccupied with the events of February 23 in the Cortes. While they gave credit to the kind and others for courageous handling of that crisis, there was general agreement that it had been a "close call."

The government of Prime Minister Calvo Sotelo had been severely tested throughout 1981. First, it had to assert political control of the government; this meant facing down hard line rightists, including the military, who believed that the democratic experiment had failed, and also Socialists and others of the Left who advocated stronger action against the plotters and their alleged supporters. Second, the government faced a deteriorating economic situation with raging inflation and very high unemployment. There can be little doubt that there was broad public support for the government's assignment of higher priority to domestic than to international affairs in that year.

On September 5, 1981, the U.S.-Spanish negotiators announced their agreement on an eight-month extension of the 1976 treaty, that is, until May 21, 1982. The official statement said the extension was needed because of the complex negotiations and "to take into account" the Spanish government's intention to join NATO. It added that the Spanish parliament was scheduled to begin debate on joining NATO later that month. [14]

The month of May 1982 became a critical one in U.S.-Spanish relations. The 1976 treaty extension was to expire on May 21, and Secretary of State Haig canceled a scheduled visit to Spain where he was expected to hammer out the last details prior to the signing of the treaty. No official reason was given for the cancellation of his trip but, according to press reports, this was due to the Falkland Islands (Malvinas) crisis in which Spain and the United States were on opposing sides. The conflict of interest in this matter incidentally raised the question of how Madrid would react in a similar situation that might involve U.S. operations against a country with which Spain was friendly. [15]

For Spain, unfortunately, the Falkland Islands issue cut both ways. Spain had been scheduled to reopen its frontier with Gibraltar on April 20, after a twelve-year closure. Simultaneously, negotiations had been scheduled to start at Sintra, Portugal, between the British and Spanish foreign ministers on the future sovereignty of the Rock. However, both sides concluded that it would be inopportune to proceed as planned, given the climate created by the Argentine takeover of the Falklands. [16] Luckily for Spain, the postponement of the Gibraltar talks came after the official invitation to join NATO had been extended. It had been announced that the Spanish-British talks would be resumed on June 25, 1982, but the continued Falklands conflict brought another postponement.

Finally, at midnight on December 14, 1982, Spain opened the border gate at La Linea. It was one of the first foreign policy moves of the new Socialist government. Premier Gonzalez called it a "humanitarian" gesture and ordered it to remain open twenty-four hours a day for Spanish citizens with valid passports and for bona fide residents of Gibraltar.[17] Tourists still could not walk or drive into Spain from Gibraltar.

On July 2, 1982, a renewal of the Pact of Madrid was quietly signed. It was downgraded from the status of a treaty to that of an executive agreement. Reportedly the negotiations were "tough." The press indicated that sharp differences arose between the defense ministry and the foreign ministry within Spain.[18] The United States was able to keep all of its bases and access to them as in the previous agreement. It may be recalled that the United States had previously agreed to take no nuclear materials into Spain after 1979. The principal U.S. concession to Spain in 1982 was $400 million of military sales, mostly F-18 planes with loan guarantees. The increased amount of economic assistance reported in the press actually was in the form of loans which Spain would probably have been able to obtain anyway.

The atmosphere surrounding the Madrid-Washington negotiations, 1981-1982, was markedly different from that of earlier renewal talks. For one thing, both sides knew Spain was soon to enter NATO. For another, the legislative concern over the agreements was centered more in the Spanish Cortes than the American Congress. On February 23, 1983, the Gonzalez government announced that it had reached agreement with the United States "to allow ratification of a five-year defense treaty permitting U.S. forces to use military bases in Spain." The announcement was made in Madrid, not Washington, and said that the pact would provide "stricter Spanish control over U.S. use of the bases."[19]

Finally, on April 20, 1983, the Cortes approved the agreement by a vote of 249-9. Prime Minister Gonzalez declared that the approval had been facilitated by an amendment to the agreement giving "Spain leeway in deciding whether to integrate its armed forces into NATO."[20]

As though to prove the point of "stricter Spanish control" mentioned above, the Spanish Minister of Defense, Narciso Serra, asserted on the day after parliamentary approval that "there are no U.S. bases in Spain," rather "there are Spanish bases which are loaned to the United States under certain conditions for certain uses, and in return for certain benefits [to Spain]."[21]

SPAIN AND THE WORLD ECONOMY

Spain's outreach after Franco was economic as well as political. The country's internal and external economic policies in the 1970s and early 1980s were steadily influenced by the expectation that Spain would joint the European Economic Community. Expectation of EEC membership also seemed to play a part in sustaining the flow of direct investment toward the economy, for foreign capital was attracted to Spain even though domestic investors became leery of soaring wage and interest costs. Yet, in 1982, negotiations for Spanish membership in the Common Market were by no means complete, and the economy remained mired in structural disequilibrium.

The EEC Application

Two weeks after its first post-Franco parliamentary elections in June 1977, Spain formally applied for full membership in the European Economic Community, the European Coal and Steel Community, and the European Atomic Energy Community. The bid followed only by months the applications of Greece and Portugal, which, with Spain, had recently improved their eligibility by the elimination of authoritarian governments. Spain's application presumably was motivated by both politics and economics—a desire for recognition among the family of western democratic states and a desire to extend preferential trading relationships with the country's well-to-do neighbors which together already took 43 percent of the country's exports. While Greece became the EEC's tenth member in 1981, the negotiations with Spain and Portugal plodded on. Spain, by far the largest of the three applicants, became the focus of the several apprehensions expressed by political groups in the EEC countries.

Some of those apprehensions were magnified by the disputes between Britain and the continental EEC members over net transfers of resources among members due to import tax collections and subsidies to producers of agricultural goods. As a major agricultural producing area, Spain seemed a candidate to be a net recipient of such transfers. More important as an obstacle in the negotiations, however, was no doubt the apprehension among French, Italian, and Greek producers of olives, wine, fruits, and vegetables concerning the effects of new competition from a large country enjoying a Mediterranean climate. Spanish fishing rights in waters of both EEC and non-EEC countries created further problems to be solved. An obstacle from the British point of view was Spain's assertion of its long-standing claim to Gibraltar and Spain's open sympathy with Argentina

TABLE 5-2

STATUS OF DOSSIERS, SPAIN-EEC NEGOTIATIONS,
DECEMBER 17, 1982

Capital movements	Agreed
Transport	Agreed
Regional policy	Agreed
Economic and financial	Agreed
Rights of establishment	Agreed
Coal and steel	In progress
External relations	In progress
Customs union	In progress
Euratom	Not begun
Harmonization of laws	In progress
Taxation	In progress
Social affairs	Not begun
Agriculture	Not begun
Fisheries	Not begun
Budget contributions	Not begun
Institutions	Not begun

Source: The Economist, December 18, 1982,
p. 58. Reprinted with permission.

in that country's 1982 contest with the British for the Falkland Islands
(Malvinas).

From Spain's perspective, the major problems of EEC membership related to whether or not membership would contribute to solution of the Gibraltar matter and whether or not Spain's young manufacturing sector could flourish in unprotected competition with EEC
producers. Issues in the application are suggested by the list of
topics that still required settlement in December 1982, shown in
Table 5-1.

The official as well as the press discussion of the economic
consequences of Spain's accession to the EEC was, and continues to
be, focused almost wholly on the disruptions to production and marketing which might arise. The truth of the matter is that it is those very
disruptions that are the potential source of gain from going ahead
with the union. The disruptions do reflect the transitional hardships
on producers as consumers avail themselves of lower-cost sources
of supply, but they also reflect the opportunities for long-run benefits.

The ultimate purpose of production is after all consumption, and the only case that can be made in favor of a country's participation in a customs union is the long-run contribution the union can make to higher consumption standards. Put succinctly, the argument in favor of the EEC's enlargement to include Spain is that it will allow Spanish consumers access to some EEC goods (for example, manufactured goods) at less cost than that at which they can be obtained in Spain, and it will allow EEC consumers greater access to those goods in Spain (for example, wine and fruit) which cost less there than elsewhere. Given a sufficiently long period of time for adjustments to be made, displaced resources in both regions will be reabsorbed in uses that the market indicates to be cost competitive. For both parties, the elimination of trade restrictions between groups <u>may</u> also make possible additional economies of scale in production in the industries which in each region increase their exports, and it <u>may</u> help disrupt producer monopoly positions. The integration of the markets, however, will in addition distort some production and consumption decisions by inducing purchases within the new union that would have been directed to low-cost producers outside had it not been for the preferential intra-group tariff treatment the union establishes. Such distortions are capable of offsetting some or all of the economic "gains" of intra-union trade creation.

Taking all possible changes into account, one cannot easily assess the long-run effects of a given union on average productivity and consumption standards. Nevertheless, in the case of Spain, in view of the substantial effective protection still provided to many Spanish industries by tariffs, quotas, and import taxes, and in view of the immense size of the North European market to which EEC membership would introduce Spanish consumers and producers, there can be little doubt that the country would reap long-term economic gains from full EEC participation. There is no doubt, too, that Western Hemisphere and Middle Eastern countries, including the United States and Spain's important Latin American and North African markets, would experience some displacement as goods moved more back and forth across the Pyrenees and less across the Atlantic. Spain's admission to the EEC will begin a new and different chapter in the economic connection between the United States and Spain.

Foreign Investment in Spain and the External Debt

The flow of direct foreign investment into Spain grew with few setbacks in a steady crescendo in the later 1970s, in spite of the depressed state of the economy and low indigenous investment. From

$325 million a year in 1975, the flow trebled to $1 billion in 1980 when it constituted between 2.5 and 3.0 percent of that year's Spanish gross fixed capital formation. There were 533 separate foreign investment projects in 1980, and 24 percent of the value of those projects was American, 17 percent Swiss, 11.8 percent French, and 11.7 percent German.[22] Massive investments in the 1970s by General Motors, Ford, Renault, Citroen, Nissan Motors, and International Harvester gave foreign firms a 59 percent stake in Spain's automobile industry. A Spanish Commerce Ministry survey of 55,746 joint stock companies reached an estimate that 8.37 percent of all Spanish corporate capital belonged to foreigners, an amount totaling $2.5 billion. Nearly a thousand subsidiaries of U.S. companies were said to be in Spain in 1982.

Spain also exploited its access to international credit markets after the petroleum crisis. Foreign and international bond issues by Spanish entities, for example, averaged $415 million per year in the three years 1978-1980, and eurocurrency borrowings were another $3.394 billion.[23] Service payments on the public foreign debt, however, were still only a modest 5.6 percent of Spanish annual exports in 1979.[24]

The international debt crisis of 1982, nonetheless, did not leave Spain unscathed. Indeed a Spanish court decision early in the year contributed to the uneasiness with which investors were beginning to view many international debts. That uneasiness was of course fully justified by the subsequent suspension of full service on the Polish, Mexican, Brazilian, and Argentine debts, among others. The decision in Spain came in January when a court disallowed the claim of foreign creditors of Immobilaria Urbis, S.A., for a judgment in dollars on a defaulted $20 million loan on grounds that dollars were not "legal tender or liquid in Spain."[25] While the creditors of Immobilaria Urbis negotiated a settlement, the case had allowed the whole matter of the collectibility of loans denominated in an international currency to be questioned.

In late September, Union Explosivos Rio Tinto, Spain's second largest private company, asked for a debt rescheduling after experiencing difficulties in refinancing its $1.6 billion debt as foreign banks began to retrench in the wake of crises in Mexico, Poland, and Argentina. Later the same week Aluminio Español, an INI-controlled aluminum company with debts of $1.4 billion, failed to make interest payments on a $200 million loan arranged by Orion Royal Bank. Aluminio is partly owned by Alugasa which is in turn 68 percent owned by Pechiney Ugine Kuhlman, recently nationalized by France, so that Aluminio's problems remained, at the close of 1982, to be sorted out among the Spanish and French governments and their foreign creditors.

THE SOCIALIST OPPORTUNITY

When the elections of October 1982 returned a Socialist government to power in Spain for the first time since the devastating civil war, the Socialists and their allies obtained an absolute majority in the Cortes. Threatened by the potentiality for violence from the Communists on the left and the military on the right, however, to say nothing of Basque and other terrorists, the Socialists had won little opportunity to make drastic change in Spain. They seemed to have little choice but to steer a course down the political middle while trying somehow to solve Spain's very difficult economic problems and make good on some of the promises of the campaign.

What the Socialists inherited was economic disorder which threatened even more than party politics to lead Spain and the Socialists to disaster. As power was transferred in November, inflation had climbed to 16 percent and was rising, unemployment had reached a similar level—some 2.1 million people and the highest proportion of the labor force since the 1930s—and was rising, a flight from the peseta was rapidly depreciating the currency despite large drawings on the foreign exchange reserves by the Bank of Spain to prop up the exchange rate, the state budget and the budget deficit were large and growing, the money supply was expanding at nearly 16 percent per annum (in September 1982), and the country's international credit was impaired by the recent failures of large Spanish borrowers to maintain their debt service. It was not an easy base from which to begin.

The Socialists unavoidably began with the depreciation of the peseta. While Bank of Spain intervention—estimated to have cost $4 billion in the year—had slowed the peseta's depreciation, the currency's decline was nonetheless from 100 to the dollar in January to 118 in November. As the Socialists took office, capital flight that was stimulated by accelerating inflation, runaway budget deficits, and inflation-portending campaign rhetoric necessitated a further retreat. On the weekend prior to Monday, December 6, the government announced that the bank's intervention rate would be raised to 127.66. In January 1983 trading was at 130.

The man named "superminister" of the combined ministries of economy, finance, and commerce in the new government was Miguel Boyer, a moderate socialist that The Economist compared to Britain's Roy Jenkins.[26] His room to maneuver was limited. To obtain anything like the promised increase in the GNP rate (from 1.2 percent in 1982 to 2.5 percent in 1983), to reduce unemployment, and to protect the balance of payments from further deterioration, he needed to restore the confidence of the investment community in Spain. Already pledged to policies encouraging wage restraint, he was pressured by business leaders also to grant employers greater flexibility in laying off workers, to avoid a temptation to balance the budget at the expense of investors, and to grant assurances there would be no emulation of French Socialist nationalization measures.

Workers, on the other hand, clearly expected further steps to redistribute income in their favor and measures to create new jobs.

The need to control inflation and to restore growth nevertheless clearly dictated that the government would have to rein in labor's demands tightly in an economic environment that was at best a zero sum game. Whether or not politics would permit such a course, however, remained to be seen as 1982 closed.

The premier said in January 1983 that Spain's government budget deficit was the equivalent of $9.35 billion, one-third larger than the previous government had forecasted, and about 4 percent of gross domestic product. Reducing government expenditures or increasing taxes, however, would slow economic activity and intensify unemployment before either could contribute to economic recovery through "supply-side" incentives. Lower real interest rates, permitted by smaller budget deficits, would, in time, stimulate private spending that would replace the shrinking contribution to the demand of declining deficits, but that, too, would probably take time.

In its election manifesto in September 1982, the Socialist Party advocated "strict price controls on basic goods." But in December Boyer denied that the government planned wage and price controls.[27]

In his first policy statement to the Cortes, Premier Gonzalez repeated his election pledge to create 800,000 new jobs in the next four years. Part of this was presumably to be achieved by further arrangements to share existing employment opportunities by reducing working hours per employee.

The Socialist government had to play for time. Each day that passed without punitive measures toward investors would increase the resolve of foreign investors to stick it out in Spain and the willingness of all savers and investors to take the actions required for new Spanish capital formation.

Furthermore, a part of the key to Spanish economic recovery did not lie in Spain itself but outside. The revival of economic activity in North America and Europe would enable Spain to have export-led recovery that would restore employment opportunities in the export sectors including tourism, rekindle opportunities and incentives for labor emigration, improve the balance of payments and strengthen the peseta, and reduce the bloated government deficits through increased tax revenues and reduced expenditures for consumption support. Fortunately, as 1983 dawned, the giant U.S. economy was yawning and stretching its limbs with signs that its worst recession since the Second World War was ending.

For Spain's Socialists, the problem was one of timing. Could internal demands for wage increases and government subsidies be postponed until external events turned favorable? Could resources that were waiting for export markets to improve meanwhile be directed to the satisfaction of domestic needs without impairing their ability again to earn foreign exchange when the opportunity came?

Sometimes a government whose devotion to the interests of one group or another is beyond doubt can influence that group to accept reality when no other government can. President Richard Nixon's recognition of the People's Republic of China was said to be such a case. As a representative of the conservative political groups that had long and adamantly opposed recognition, Nixon was able to take the step that no Democratic president had been able to carry through. The Socialist government in Spain has a somewhat parallel opportunity. If that government can use its stock of good will with workers to persuade them to live realistically at mildly declining real wages for months or a year or more, and if it meanwhile uses the interim to dampen internal inflation forces stemming from monetary growth and the ballooning budget deficits, it may be rewarded with a somewhat brighter outlook and with greater flexibility of action in its second and third years in power.

It is of course unlikely that the Communist-led unions will make such a waiting game easy, and they may make it impossible. It is, nonetheless, the only practical strategy available. If the Communists along with left-leaning Socialists, succeed in stampeding the government into rash action, the government will then find itself reacting to crises by emergency regulations on the foreign exchange markets, by wage and price controls, by efforts to get jobs started through public investments funded with inflationary bank credit, and possibly by returning to a policy of selective nationalization of firms or industries. Such emergency efforts, undertaken in circumstances in which alarmed owners of private property would be seeking capital preservation, would have no near term change of regenerating growth or removing the distortions of inflation, and they might, in any case, provoke the political right into restoration of a military rule. There is only a razor-thin path for the Spanish Socialists to follow, and it is not one to their liking.

Fortunately, the Socialists have on degree of freedom in policy action. They may be able to make a good show of social reforms in education (where, however, they must be careful not to overly upset the church), in health (again, the church and traditionalists will be resistive), in legal processes, and in civil services; in the process they may temporarily divert attention from some of the hard core economic issues. The party was elected to bring about "the change" (from the establishment held over after Franco), and if they seize their opportunity they may be able to focus on social reform until the environment improves for economic progress.

Both the United States and Western Europe have a keen interest in the outcome of the Spanish political-economic drama. The United States of course would like continued access to the military bases it constructed there, and, on behalf of some of its citizens it has an interest in the security of U.S. investments in Spain. But much more important, it has a deep concern for the preservation of democratic institutions in Spain. For in the thirty-year "connection," the cultivation of conditions for the emergence and survival of such freedoms has played a role at least equal to that of perceived international security needs in motivating the American people and their governments in relation to the people of Spain.

Spain's connection with the United States in the early 1980s was being replaced by a connection with Europe, and as that linkage strengthened, Europe, too, could not be insensitive to developments in Spain. Indeed, any failure of democracy in Spain would inevitably waft radical ideas across Europe which would be threatening to both economic and political stability.

Democracy, manifesting widespread political liberty, is always an exciting game with high stakes, but it is not necessarily a tough or durable institution. In Spain it may be unstable. Still, its flowering in the late 1970s and early 1980s, as a result of cultivation by Spaniards and their friends abroad, may be so much revered that the institution will escape disassembly in the middle third of the 1980s. The sense of political responsibility that inevitably arises in a newly entrenched middle class may be a factor in enabling democracy to survive, for a great number of Spaniards now have a great deal to lose from a threat to democratic government. If survive it does, Spanish democracy will be a brilliant memorial to the diplomacy that was the cement of a historic thirty-year special connection between Spain and the United States.

CONCLUSION

While the more publicized events of history swirled in and out of the headlines over the past three decades, the United States and Spain found common cause in the base agreements. Neither party was ever fully satisfied. Each made sizable concessions to the other. In the showdown they could forget other differences and unite in their determination to stand firm against the threat from the East. Through the

U.S.-Spanish connection the other members of NATO, for 20 years, had the benefit of Spain's strategic location without bearing the onus of "dealing with Franco."

Experts can argue whether the U.S.-Spanish connection was on the margin of history or in its mainstream. Some results, however, are unarguable. The United States had access to Spanish bases when it could no longer use those in France, Morocco, and Libya. Moreover, eight American presidents—Truman, Eisenhower, Kennedy, Johnson, Nixon, Ford, Carter, and Reagan—as well as the U.S. Congress, thought Spain important enough to the U.S. defense system to renew the base agreements and to cooperate in the economic modernization and development of Spain. As for Spain, it had the public support of the United States when all other doors were closed.

The true significance of the American connection with Spain was both in its timing and in its substance. The connection arose in 1953 when Spain was desperately in need. It served then as a catalyst to Spain's use of its own resources, bringing economic relief and hope to the Spanish people. The United States was in pursuit of strategic advantages which it perceived to be vital. The synergistic effect of the connection was beneficial to both nations.

Socrates wrote "let him that would move the world first move himself." The United States has tried twice in the twentieth century to "move the world" by joining extensive military actions in which it was not an initial participant. First, it wanted to make "the world safe for democracy." Thirty years later it tried to undergird the "four freedoms" for mankind. While neither effort ended in abject failure, neither produced the hoped-for better world. The American connection with Spain was just one small move on the worldwide strategy board, but it was an important part of the game. Spain, three centuries ago, also tried "to move the world." After that effort failed, Spain reverted to a smaller role, almost succeeding in isolating itself behind the Pyrenees. But neither tyranny nor war destroyed its spirit. Finally, in 1953, with its American connection to the postwar world, Spain began to "move itself." It has succeeded beyond expectations.

The United States has already learned that it is dealing with a Spain different from before. Rather than being a monolithic government, today's Spanish government is in place by virtue of popular vote which can remove those in power as fast as it seated them. Just as Spaniards had to learn to adapt to the "many faces of America," so Americans are now having to identify and adapt to the "many faces of Spain."

Spain truly is a kaleidoscopic scene. The Madrid government is a case in point. In seven years it has been headed by four prime ministers whose political orientation has ranged from Francoist right to Socialist left.

The information media offer another example. While one might have expected a completely unrestricted press after so many years of censorship, most visitors to Spain are surprised by the extent to which "anything goes" in both the electronic and print media.

No more exhilarating "face of Spain" is likely to be encountered by visitors than that reflected by Spanish scholars. Economists, political scientists, historians, sociologists, lawyers, doctors, artists, and journalists—not to exhaust the list—all seem to have a wideranging intellectual curiosity.

One common trait stands out. Spaniards generally seem willing to accept responsibility for what their country is today and what it is to be in the future. There is surprisingly little "scapegoating."

Some cautions are in order. In Spain one notices the generation gap between those who lived under Franco, and those who either have forgotten those times or were too young to remember. The young never seem to look back. But that recent history must either be remembered or learned, if that lesson is not to have to be repeated. As Salvador Madariaga wrote, "The chief need of the Spanish people is to learn to create order."[28] They will be rich if they learn to create it without repression.

The pressures that brought Spain and the United States together in 1953 are unlikely to recur, but the years beyond 1983 will provide new opportunities for close cooperation. Neither country needs the other in the 1980s as it did in the 1950s, yet each side seems to want the other. If the U.S.-Spanish connection endures for another three decades, it will be because both sides want it. It will be because each has earned the respect of the other and has grown in understanding.

NOTES

1. Juan Goytisolo, quoted in Alistair Reid's New Yorker article, February 1979.

2. David C. Jordan, Spain, The Monarchy and the Atlantic Community, Institute for Foreign Policy Analysis, Inc., Monograph, June 1979, p. 3.

3. Ibid.

4. ABC (Madrid), March 23, 1976.

5. Ibid., June 10, 1976.

6. Jordan, Spain, The Monarchy and the Atlantic Community, p. 6.

7. Javier Garcia Fernandez, "La Constitución Expresión de la Ruptura Pactada," Triuno, January 7, 1978, pp. 14-15.

8. Jordan, Spain, The Monarchy and the Atlantic Community, p. 46.

9. Ibid., p. 30.

10. Arnold Hottinger, Spain in Transition: Franco's Regime, Sage Policy Paper (Beverly Hills, London, 1974), pp. 30-32.

11. Tad Szulc, "The Politics of Church-State Relations in Spain," in William T. Salisbury and James D. Theberge, eds., Spain in the 1970s (New York: Praeger, 1976), p. 64.

12. Jordan, Spain, The Monarchy and the Atlantic Community, p. 44.

13. Fernando Moran, "Nato and Defense Scenarios Which Affect Spain," Social Science Review (March 1980): 142.

14. Dallas Morning News, September 8, 1981.

15. Ibid., December 7, 1981.

16. Christian Science Monitor, May 19, 1982.

17. Ibid., April 9, 1982.

18. Dallas Morning News, December 15, 1982.

19. Ibid., February 24, 1983.

20. Wall Street Journal, April 21, 1983.

21. Excelsior, Mexico City, April 23, 1983.

22. Spanish Ministry of Commerce, cited in World Business Weekly, April 13, 1981, p. 34.

23. World Bank Annual Report, 1981, pp. 145, 147.

24. Ibid., Table 4, p. 139.

25. Wall Street Journal, February 1, 1982.

26. The Economist, December 4, 1982.

27. Wall Street Journal, December 6, 1982.

28. Salvador Madariaga, Spain, A Modern History (New York: Praeger, 1958), pp. 642-43.

Index

159

International Telecommunications
Union, 21
International Telephone and Telegraph
Company, 21
Israel, 58, 106-7
isolationism, Spanish, 5
Italy, 10

Japan, 129
Johnson, Lyndon, 88, 153
Johnson, U. Alexis, 82, 93, 94
Joint Consultative Committee on
Defense Matters, 83
Jordan, 58
Juan Carlos (King of Spain), 91, 108,
113-14, 118, 134, 135
JUSMAAG, 34, 79
JUSMG, 34

Kaplan, Stephen S., 58
Karramanlis, 110
Kennedy, John, 79, 81, 153
Kennedy, Joseph P., Jr., 81
Kissinger, Henry, 89, 107, 114, 115-17
Kissner, August W., 22, 26
Korean War, 2, 3, 16, 20

Labor Party (British), 59
labor relations, 7-8
labor unions, 122, 123-25, 136, 151
language facility, 38
La Souchere, Elena de, 13
Latin America, 2, 11, 13, 59, 63, 140
Law for the Protection of Industry, 6
layoffs, 8
LeMay, Curtis, 82
Lequerica, José Felix, 10
Libya, 92
Llorca, Perez, 142
Lodge, John Davis, 40
Lopez Bravo, Gregorio, 91, 92
Lopez Rodo, Laureano, 67, 107

McCarran, Patrick, 11, 14, 19, 20, 40,
42, 55, 72
McCarthy, Joseph, 15
McCloskey, Robert, 111-12, 115, 118-19

McVeigh, Lincoln, 22, 26
Madariaga, Salvador de, 2, 154
Madrid, Pact of, 2-3, 31, 40, 43, 54,
71; renewals, 82-83, 86-94, 142-44
Madrid, University of, 38
Madrid Vatican Concordats, 24-25,
135, 139
Makarios, 110
Mallorca, 36
manufacturing, 6
Mao Zedong, 13. See also People's
Republic of China
Marshall Plan. See European Recovery
Program
Martínez Méndez, Pedro, 126, 127
Meany, George, 56
merchant marine, 4
mercury, 21
Mexico, 63
Milans de Bosch, Jaime, 142
Mitterand, François, 137
Molina, Antonio Tejero, 141
Moncloa, Pact of, 122
Moran, Fernando, 118, 140
Morocco, 35, 58, 60-61, 87
Morón de la Frontera air base, 34, 52,
91
Morrison, Herbert, 3
Movement, the, 134, 136
Mutual Defense Assistance Agreement,
32, 33
Mutual Security Act of 1951, 32, 33
Mutual Security Agency, 45

National Aeronautics and Space Admin-
istration, 84
National Catholic Welfare Conference,
45
National Development Plans, 94
National Economic Council (Spanish), 4
National Industrial Productivity Service,
53
National Institute of Colonization, 6
National Movement, 134, 136
National Security Council, 15, 17
National Socialism (German), 65
NATO. See North Atlantic Treaty
Organization
naval bases, 11, 18, 22-23, 26-27,
34-36

Viñas, Angel, 41, 45

wages, 123-25
Walsh Construction Company, 35
War Powers Act, 94
Washington Post, 84
Weeks, Stanley B., 79
Welles, Benjamin, 36, 79, 82
Wheat Institute, 19
Wheeler, Earle, 86, 88, 89
Wheelus Air Base (Libya), 92
Whitaker, Arthur P., 13, 23, 34, 56
Williams, Edward, 37
Wilson, Harold, 59

Wohlstetter, Albert, 56
Wilson, James, 15, 17
Woodward, 80
Workers' Commissions (CCOO), 124
World Bank, 65, 68, 95, 96, 101
World Health Organization, 21, 59
World War II, 4, 63

Yugoslavia, 14

Zablocki, 11
Zaragoza Air Base, 36, 52, 92
zinc, 4

About the Authors

R. RICHARD RUBOTTOM is a Professor Emeritus of Political Science at Southern Methodist University. He retired from the U.S. Foreign Service in 1964 in the rank of Career Minister, after serving as Assistant Secretary of State for Inter-American Affairs, 1956-1960, and as Ambassador to Argentina in 1960-1961. During his career as a naval officer during World War II, and as a Foreign Service officer, he was assigned to posts in Mexico, Paraguay, Colombia, Spain, and Argentina.

Rubottom became Vice-President of Southern Methodist University in 1964, serving in that capacity until 1971, when he assumed the presidency of the University of the Americas, in Puebla, Mexico.

J. CARTER MURPHY received his Ph.D. from the University of Chicago in 1955. He has had extensive experience in the economic policy making and academic fields. He is the author or editor of two books on the international monetary system and numerous journal articles. He has served as senior staff member of the President's Council of Economic Advisors, special field representative for the Rockefeller Foundation in Thailand, Fulbright Scholar in Denmark and Italy, and U.N. Technical Assistance Expert in Egypt.

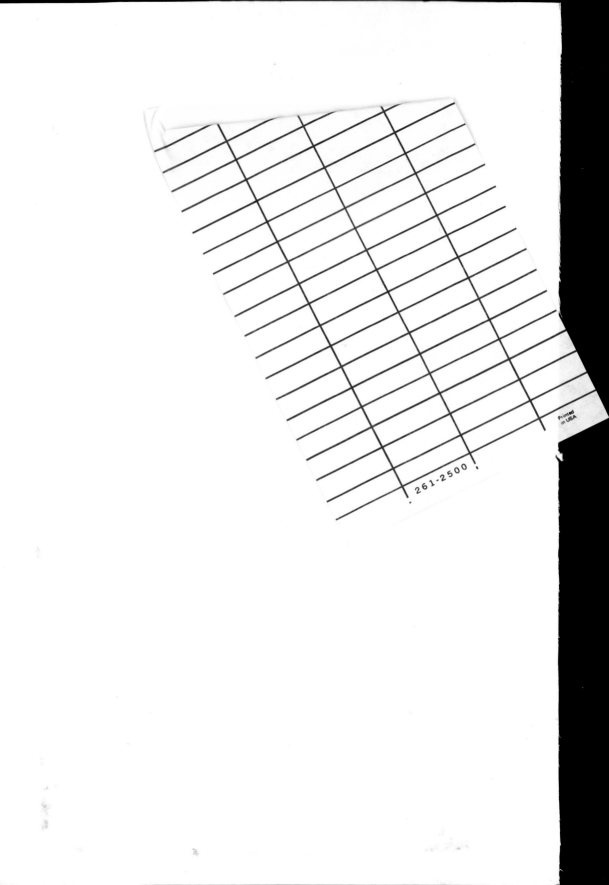

261-2500

Printed
in USA